OXFORD
UNIVERSITY PRESS

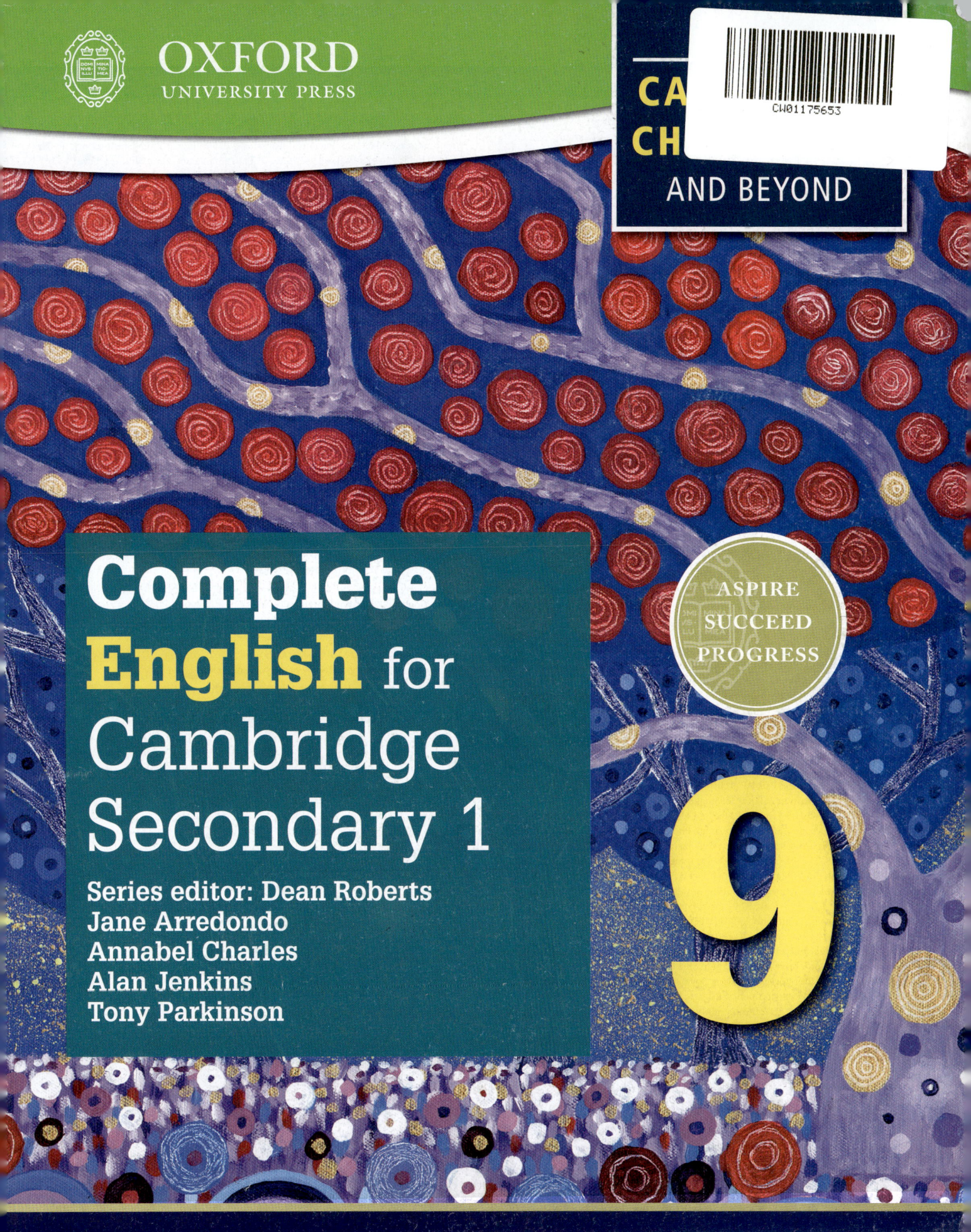

AND BEYOND

Complete English for Cambridge Secondary 1

9

ASPIRE
SUCCEED
PROGRESS

Series editor: Dean Roberts
Jane Arredondo
Annabel Charles
Alan Jenkins
Tony Parkinson

Oxford excellence for Cambridge Secondary 1

OXFORD

OXFORD
UNIVERSITY PRESS

Great Clarendon Street, Oxford, OX2 6DP, United Kingdom

Oxford University Press is a department of the University of Oxford.
It furthers the University's objective of excellence in research, scholarship,
and education by publishing worldwide. Oxford is a registered trade mark of Oxford
University Press in the UK and in certain other countries

© Oxford University Press 2016

The moral rights of the authors have been asserted

First published in 2016

All rights reserved. No part of this publication may be reproduced, stored in a retrieval system, or transmitted, in any form or by any means, without the prior permission in writing of Oxford University Press, or as expressly permitted by law, by licence or under terms agreed with the appropriate reprographics rights organization. Enquiries concerning reproduction outside the scope of the above should be sent to the Rights Department, Oxford University Press, at the address above.

You must not circulate this work in any other form and you must impose this same condition on any acquirer

British Library Cataloguing in Publication Data
Data available

978-0-19-836467-2

10 9 8 7 6 5 4

Paper used in the production of this book is a natural, recyclable product made from wood grown in sustainable forests.
The manufacturing process conforms to the environmental regulations of the country of origin.

Printed in India by Manipal Technologies Limited

Acknowledgements

The publishers would like to thank the following for permissions to use their photographs:

Cover image: David Newton/Bridgeman Art; P2: mrmohock/Shutterstock; P2l: Samuel Borges Photography/Shutterstock; P2r: Directphoto Collection/Alamy Stock Photo; P3: Britta Pedersen/dpa/Corbis/Image Library; P4: Ming-Hsiang Chuang/Shutterstock; P7: Eric Isselee/Shutterstock; P12: c.Warner Br/Everett/REX Shutterstock; ScotStock/Alamy Stock Photo; P17: Dragon Images/Shutterstock; P16: Indeed/Getty Images; P20: Merlin74/Shutterstock; P20l: microgen/iStock; P20r: Patrick Aventurier/Getty Images; P21: Albert Moldvay/National Geographic/Getty Images; P22: Tribune Content Agency LLC/Alamy Stock Photo; P23: Lacovara Lab, Drexel University; P30: University of Leices/Demotix/Corbis/Image Library; P31: GL Archive/Alamy Stock Photo; P32: wawritto/Shutterstock; P33: wavebreakmedia/Shutterstock; P34: Robert Frerck/Getty Images; P35: Arterra Picture Library/Alamy Stock Photo; P38: Fredrick Kippe/Alamy Stock Photo; P38l: Aija Lehtonen/Shutterstock; P38r: Frank Trapper/Corbis/Image Library; P39t: ev radin/Shutterstock; P39m: The Asahi Shimbun/Getty Images; P39b: Matthias Oesterle/ZUMA Press/Corbis/Image Library; P40: AF archive/Alamy Stock Photo; P41: Mati Nitibhon/Shutterstock; P44: Naashon Zalk/Corbis/Image Library; P45: Pacific Press/Corbis/Image Library; P49: Corbis/Image Library; P51: Blaj Gabriel/Shutterstock; P52t: Photos 12/Alamy Stock Photo; P52b: Lumi Images/Alamy Stock Photo; P54: Christopher Futcher/Getty Images; P56: Vertyr/Shutterstock; P56l: potowizard/Shutterstock; P56r: Production Perig/Shutterstock; P58: The Asahi Shimbun/Getty Images; P59: The Asahi Shimbun/Getty Images; P60: Akio Kon/Bloomberg/Getty Images; P62: MEGiordano_Photography/iStock; P64: PeopleImages/Getty Images; P68: Hemis/Alamy Stock Photo; P70: www.nasa.gov; P72: Scott Bedford/Shutterstock; P74: siiixth/Shutterstock; P74l: Castleski/Shutterstock; P74r: Osadchaya Olga/Shutterstock; P75: MuchMania/Shutterstock; P78: Robbie Shone/Aurora Photos/Corbis/Image Library; P80: Daisy Gilardini/Getty Images; P84: Peter McBride/Aurora Photos/Corbis/Image Library; P85: Susan Montgomery/Shutterstock; P86: John W Banagan/Getty Images; P90: sergign/Shutterstock; P91: Brian Bailey/Getty Images; P92: BABAROGA/Shutterstock; P92l: Yuriy Boyko/Shutterstock; P92r: ALBERTO PIZZOLI/AFP/Getty Images; P93: Martin Good/Shutterstock; P94: Lukas Gojda/Shutterstock; P95: Kamira/Shutterstock; P97: Ensuper/Shutterstock; P98: ascal Le Segretain/Sygma/Corbis/Image Library; P99: PHILIPPE DESMAZES/AFP/Getty Images; P100: retrorocket/Shutterstock; P101: Ola-ola/Shutterstock; P102l: Matthew Willman/Gallo Images/Getty Images; P102r: Christy Bowe/Corbis/Image Library; P107: TashaNatasha/Shutterstock; P110: jeep2499/Shutterstock; P110l: D and D Photo Sudbury/Shutterstock; P110r: Helen E. Grose/Shutterstock; P111: Scott E Read/Shutterstock; P112: small1/Shutterstock; P113: Ging o_o/Shutterstock; P116: The Tyger', plate 36 (Bentley 42) from 'Songs of Innocence and of Experience' (Bentley Copy 1) 1789-94 (relief etching with pen & w/c), Blake, William (1757-1827)/Yale Center for British Art, Paul Mellon Collection, USA/Bridgeman Images; P119: Zurijeta/Shutterstock; P120: Willyam Bradberry/Shutterstock; P124: Nneirda/Shutterstock; P126/127: dangdumrong/Shutterstock; P128: CEBImagery.com/Shutterstock; P128l: Tukaram Karve/Shutterstock; P128r: Andrzej Kubik/Shutterstock; P130: Earl D. Walker/Shutterstock; P132: Zdenek Rosenthaler/Shutterstock; P133: Richard Bickel/CORBIS/Image Library; P134: SIHASAKPRACHUM/Shutterstock; P135t: loca4motion/Shutterstock; P135b: Creativa Images/Shutterstock; P138: Bananaboy/Shutterstock; P143: Mike Richter/Shutterstock; P144: Andrzej Wilusz/Shutterstock; P146: gsjha/Shuttersock; P146l: Olga Danylenko/Shutterstock; P146r: Image Source Plus/Alamy Stock Photo; P147: Oleg Zabielin/Shutterstock; P148l: Hill Street Studios/Getty Images; P148r: ONTHEBIKE.PL/Alamy Stock Photo; P151: mikecphoto/Shutterstock; P155: edella/Shutterstock; P156: RosaIreneBetancourt 7/Alamy Stock Photo; P157: RosaIreneBetancourt 7/Alamy Stock Photo; P160: Ivica Drusany/Shutterstock; P163t: Merkushev Vasiliy/Shutterstock; P163b: Greg Epperson/Shutterstock; P164: 06photo/Shutterstock; P164l: Sean Pavone/Shutterstock; P164r: Ingvar Bjork/Shutterstock; P165t: Poprotskiy Alexey/Shutterstock; P165b: OUP; P166: macumazahn/Shutterstock; P167t: imageBROKER/Alamy Stock Photo; P167b: Elena Lebedeva-Hooft/Shutterstock; P168: S.Borisov/Shutterstock; P169: IM_photo/Shutterstock; P170: Sentavio/Shutterstock; P171t: Volodymyr Goinyk/Shutterstock; P171b: Credit: Cultura RM Exclusive/Lost Horizon Images/Getty Images.

Artwork by Six Red Marbles and OUP.

The author and publisher are grateful for permission to reprint extracts from the following copyright material:

Isabel Allende: *City of the Beasts* (*La ciudad de las bestias*) translated by Margaret Sayers Peden (Flamingo, 2003), copyright © Isabel Allende 2002, translation copyright © Margaret Sayers Peden 2002, reprinted by permission of HarperCollins Publishers Ltd, and the Agencia Literaria Carmen Balcells S A.

Bill Bryson: *Notes from A Big Country: Journey into the American Dream* (Doubleday, 1998), copyright © Bill Bryson 1998, reprinted by permission of the Random House Group Ltd; published in the USA as *I'm a Stranger Here Myself: Notes on returning to America after twenty years away* (Doubleday, 1999), copyright © Bill Bryson 1999, reprinted by permission of Broadway Books, an imprint of the Crown Publishing Group, a division of Penguin Random House LLC. All rights reserved.

Angela Clarence: 'Children of the Stars', *The Observer*, 5 Nov 2000, copyright © Guardian News and Media Ltd, 2000 reprinted by permission of GNM Ltd.

Danielle Demetriou: 'Robot Hotel, Inside Japan's Henn na Hotel', *Daily Telegraph*, 16 July 2015, Copyright © Telegraph Media Group Ltd 2015, reprinted by permission of TMG.

Franz Kafka: *Metamorphosis* from *The Metamorphosis and Other Stories* translated by Joyce Crick (Oxford World Classics, 2009), translation copyright © Joyce Crick 2009, reprinted by permission of Oxford University Press.

Denise Levertov: 'To the Snake', copyright © Denise Levertov 1958, from *New Selected Poems* (Bloodaxe, 2003), reprinted by permission of Bloodaxe Books Ltd; also from *Collected Earlier Poems 1940-1960* (New Directions, 1960), copyright © Denise Levertov 1960, reprinted by permission of New Directions Publishing Corp.

Geraldine McCaughrean: *The Kite Rider* (OUP, 2007), copyright © Geraldine McCaughrean 2001, reprinted by permission of Oxford University Press.

James Vance Marshall: *Walkabout* (Puffin, 2009), first published as *The Children*, copyright © James Vance Marshall 1959, reprinted by permission of the publishers, Penguin Books Ltd, Sundance Newbridge LLC, and of Johnson & Alcock Ltd.

Sylvia Plath: 'Medallion' from *The Colossus* (Faber, 1960), copyright © Sylvia Plath 1957, 1958, 1959, 1960, 1961, 1962, reprinted by permission of the publishers, Faber & Faber Ltd and Alfred A Knopf, an imprint of the Knopf Doubleday Publishing Group, a division of Penguin Random House LLC. All rights reserved.

Ian Sample: 'Battleship beast: colossal dinosaur skeleton found in southern Patagonia', *The Guardian*, 4 July 2014, copyright © Guardian News and Media Ltd 2014, reprinted by permission of GNM Ltd.

Mandy Sinclair: 'A Sunday Morning in Ait Bougmez' from *Why Morocco*, 26 April 2015, at www.whymorocco.wordpress.com.

and to the following for permission to reprint copyright material:

The Associated Press via the YGS Group for extract from 'France recreates prehistoric paintings from disputed Chauvet Cave', 10 April 2015, copyright © The Associated Press 2015.

Cable News Network (CNN) for extract from 'First man to hike Amazon River ends 2-year, 4000-mile trek', 10 Aug 2010, copyright © CNN 2010.

Exodus Travels Ltd for advertisement for Antarctica expedition.

Responsible Travel for advertisement 'Come and experience a Peru Amazon Rainforest family adventure!' from www.responsibletravel.com.

Virgin Holidays for advertisement 'New York city holiday' 4 from www.virginholidays.co.uk

World Challenge for extracts from their website www.world-challenge.co.uk.

Any third party use of this material, outside of this publication, is prohibited. Interested parties should apply to the copyright holders indicated in each case.

Although we have made every effort to trace and contact all copyright holders before publication this has not been possible in all cases. If notified, the publisher will rectify any errors or omissions at the earliest opportunity.

®IGCSE is the registered trademark of Cambridge International Examinations.

All sample questions and answers within this publication have been written by the authors. In examination, the way marks are awarded may be different.

Contents

Introduction iv

1 **Alternative reality** 2
Learning about narrative viewpoint, understanding archaic language; punctuation in complex sentences, using embedded clauses; talking about film; writing a fantasy story

2 **Dramatic discoveries** 20
Non-fiction: examining the past; creating a drama script; combining words; writing a summary

3 **Fame** 38
Discussing famous people; making adjectives; writing a television script; group role-playing activities

4 **Leisure and travel** 56
Non-fiction: travel writing, creating a humorous tone; using juxtaposition and oxymoron; hyperbole; creating a travel blog

5 **Exhilarating exploration!** 74
Examining different text types; identifying figurative language; varying sentence structure; writing a travel brochure

6 **Rights and freedom** 92
Using topic sentences; understanding abstract nouns; using discourse markers; presenting an effective argument

7 **Poetic predators** 110
Creating a group poem; comparing different poems; writing from notes; punctuation; using poetic imagery; expressing an opinion

8 **People and places** 128
Fiction: presenting character, describing places and lifestyles; using compound sentences; responding to narratives

9 **Challenge!** 146
Revising listening, reading and writing skills including inference, planning, punctuation; using language to convey meaning; non-narrative writing task

10 **Pathways – going places** 164
Non-fiction: travel writing, writing to persuade; creating a holiday advertisement

Extended reading: *The Kite Rider* by Geraldine McCaughrean 172

Language and literacy reference 178

Introduction to Student Book 9

In this Stage 9 book you will explore themes and topics such as fame, leisure, nature, alternative realities, exploration and discoveries, different cultures, rights and freedom, and challenges. There is also a *Pathways* unit which helps you make the transition from previous learning towards more formal examinations of your knowledge, skills and understanding. In addition, there is a revision unit (Unit 9 *Challenge!*) which revisits some key skills in reading, writing, listening and speaking that you have been developing all the way back from Stage 7.

In Stage 9, we have focused on a single theme for each unit and our aim is to develop your reading, writing, listening and speaking skills with a range of interactive and hands-on activities based on that theme.

Reading

You will read about a character in literature called Gregor, who one morning after a troubled night woke up not as a human! This extract will help you learn about how narrative works, and in particular, how a writer controls the narrative. You'll also read about a drought in Trinidad and how it affected the local people. Here, you will learn about how writers choose their descriptive words with care. A different kind of reading will also introduce you to a real-life explorer who walked the entire length of the Amazon river, and it took over 2 years. And you'll also read poems about sharks, snakes and tigers! If you like history, you will also enjoy reading about Richard the Third.

Word cloud / Glossary

Use the Word clouds to learn new vocabulary, exploring meanings and usage in context. The Glossary features will help you with words or phrases that you may not find in a dictionary because they are uncommon, colloquial or technical phrases.

Listening

You will listen to: a talk about the early life of Nelson Mandela, a discussion where four students talk about their very different cultural backgrounds, a lively discussion where two people debate if the book is always better than the film and a radio broadcast about the discovery of the bones of an English King who died hundreds of years ago. When you listen to all of these people, and more, you will be practising your skills of listening to locate details, listening to understand the gist of what is being said and listening to make inferences – trying to work out what people really mean!

Writing

You will write a wide range of pieces: a persuasive essay, arguing whether you should be allowed to listen to music while you study at school, a review of some new poems, a travel brochure advertising a holiday on a remote and exotic island, a television screenplay about a detective trying to solve a crime, a story based on a character you have created, and a summary based on an article of how best to get a good night's sleep! Each of these writing tasks is part of a writing workshop where you will be given ideas and advice about how to construct the writing in stages.

Speaking

We believe that dialogic learning is really important. *Dialogic* means learning through talking a lot! You will take part in a wide range of speaking contexts, sometimes talking by yourself, other times working with a partner, but also taking part in small group discussions. Learning how and when to make your contributions is a key skill for success in your future examinations, but also in life. Some of the speaking tasks are: a group poetry game, reading some poems out loud by yourself, a discussion about which roles each member of your group will play as you set off to walk the Amazon river on an expedition, working out with a partner what is it about famous people that help them become famous, being in the hot seat as a famous person, role-playing a music agent who spots a new singing star, giving a multi-media presentation about the place where you live, and playing your part in a range of dramatic pieces.

Language development

When the opportunities arise, we have incorporated language learning activities for you. We hope that these language awareness and language development activities will help improve your grammar, spelling and punctuation. In this Stage 9 book there is a focus on using topic sentences to good effect, abstract nouns, transition and connecting words, using discourse markers in speech which are better than *um* or *er*, choosing adjectives carefully, getting to grips with complex sentences by experimenting with punctuation, making sure you use a wider range of sentence types in your writing than you have before, and exploring words that end in *tic*.

Vocabulary

Learning new words and perhaps more importantly, learning exactly how they should be used is a key element of this series of books. There are lots of *word building* exercises for you to extend and enhance your vocabulary. Some new words you will meet in Stage 9 are: sonata, plausible, pliable, affiliation, opaque, glinting, serrated, douse, adversary, conjecture, limelight, philanthropy, parched, desolation, forage, inhospitable, foray, and eradicate. Well done if you already know some of these. Don't worry if you don't – it's our aim to help you build up your vocabulary.

Moving towards formal assessment

In this Stage 9 book we have introduced a new section at the end of each unit which aims to help you practise the skills you will need for your Cambridge Secondary 1 Checkpoint test. Every unit invites you to self-assess and reflect on your own learning by presenting you with some questions like the ones you will find in the test. There are also sample student responses (written by the authors) which you can explore and even mark. In addition, there are some useful tips for you to improve in key skills areas.

1 Alternative reality

Explore
- alternative realities
- the land of Lilliput

Create
- fantasy fiction story
- a compelling opening paragraph

Engage
- in a discussion on books and films
- in understanding other people's points of view

Collaborate
- on grammar practice
- on finding the meaning of old-fashioned words and expressions

In this unit you will:

Reflect
- on how authors create main characters
- on how we read what other people have written

"Reading is to the mind what exercise is to the body."
Sir Richard Steele

"'and what is the use of a book,' thought Alice, 'without pictures or conversation?'"
Lewis Carroll, Alice's Adventures in Wonderland

"I think you should only read those books which bite and sting you."
Franz Kafka

Thinking time

1. In what ways does reading exercise the mind?
2. Do we need illustrations in books to see what the characters look like? Why?
3. Look at the third quotation. How can a book 'bite' or 'sting' you?

Types of novels – fiction genres

Here is a list of popular fiction genres:

children's — M, CF, JB
young adult (YA) — LOR
fantasy — Alice, HP
romance
science-fiction — META

crime (murder mystery) — SH
thriller
adventure — FT, C OF THE WILD, White Fang
historical
westerns — RBC

Answer these questions, explaining your views as fully as possible.

1. Which genre(s) do you prefer? Explain why.
2. Which sort of novel(s) would you never choose in a library or book shop? Why?

Speaking and listening

Talk about a film you have seen which is based on a book you know. Answer these questions.

1. Were the characters in the film better than the characters in the book?
2. What makes a movie character memorable?
3. Can you think of a character in a book who reminds you of a real person? Explain why, or why not.
4. Why may characters in films sometimes be confused with the actors who play them?
5. Think about how young people of your age may have lived during the past, before cinema and television had been invented. Discuss:
   a what they did for entertainment
   b what books they may have read and why.
6. Do you think reading for entertainment will be something future generations will do? Explain your answer.

Alternative reality

📖 Metamorphosis

1   As Gregor Samsa woke one morning from uneasy dreams, he found himself transformed into some kind of monstrous **vermin**. He lay on his hard, armour-like back, and if he lifted his head a little, he could see his curved brown **abdomen**, divided by
5   arch-shaped ridges, and domed so high that the **bedspread**, on the brink of slipping off, could hardly stay put. His many legs, **miserably** thin in comparison with his size otherwise, flickered helplessly before his eyes.

'What has happened to me?' he thought. It was not a dream.
10   His room, a proper human being's room, rather too small, lay peacefully between its four familiar walls. (…)

Gregor's gaze then turned towards the window, and the **murky** weather—one could hear the raindrops striking the **window-sill**—made him quite **melancholy**. 'What if I went on sleeping
15   for a while and forgot all these **idiocies**?', he thought, but that was quite impossible, as he was used to sleeping on his right side and in his present state he was unable to get himself into this position. However energetically he flung himself onto his right side, whenever he did so he would rock onto his back again. He
20   must have tried a hundred times, shutting his eyes so that he didn't have to see his **jittery** legs, and he only gave over when he began to feel a slight ache in his side, something he had never felt before. (…)

He felt a slight itching high on his abdomen. He pushed himself
25   slowly on his back towards the bedpost so that he could lift his head more easily; he found the itching spot, which was covered with lots of little white dots he had no idea how to interpret. He tried to probe the spot with one of his legs, but drew back at once, for the moment he touched it he was swept by cold shivers. (…)

30   Throwing off the bedspread was quite simple; he needed only to puff himself up a little and it fell down of its own accord. But after that it got difficult, particularly because he was so uncommonly wide. He would have needed arms and hands to raise himself; but instead of those, he had only these many little
35   legs, which were continually fluttering about, and which he could not control anyhow. If he tried to bend one of them, it was

Word cloud
abdomen	melancholy
bedspread	miserably
idiocy	murky
jittery	vermin
mass	window-sill

Glossary
had no idea how to interpret was not sure about or did not know what to think

swept by cold shivers to start trembling

wide being of great or more than average width

at any price under any circumstances

the first to stretch; and if he finally managed to get this leg to do what he wanted, all the others were flapping about meanwhile in the most intense and painful excitement, as if they had been let
40 loose. (…)

So he attempted to get his upper body out of the bed first, cautiously turning his head towards the edge. This worked easily enough, and in the end, despite its width and weight, the **mass** of his body slowly followed the way his head was turning.
45 But when at last he held his head in the air outside the bed, he became afraid of moving any further forward in this way, for if he did finally let himself drop, it would need a sheer miracle for his head to remain unharmed. And right now was no time to lose consciousness, not at any price; he would sooner stay in bed.

from *Metamorphosis* by Franz Kafka

Understanding

Answer the following questions.

1. Why can't Gregor get out of bed?
   Write one sentence in your own words. Give a quotation from the passage to support your answer.

2. Suggest what type of 'vermin' Gregor has turned into.

3. In the last paragraph, Gregor becomes afraid. What is he afraid of, and why?

4. Explain in your own words what Gregor might be thinking in the final sentence: 'And right now was no time to lose consciousness, not at any price; he would sooner stay in bed.'

5. From whose point of view does the author tell the story? Give a reason to support your answer.

6. In the second paragraph the author says 'It was not a dream.'
   a In your opinion, why does he tell the reader this?
   b What effect does this have on how we read the rest of the extract?

Alternative reality

Key concept

Narrative viewpoint

This extract from *Metamorphosis* is written in the *third person*, using Gregor's name and 'he'. The author, Franz Kafka, uses an *omniscient narrator* who knows everything that is happening, but he is writing from Gregor's *point of view*.

If you are writing someone's thoughts you can put them in quotation marks. Quotation marks around a character's thoughts go into the main body of a paragraph. Quotation marks in a dialogue should start a new line, indenting the first word for each new person speaking.

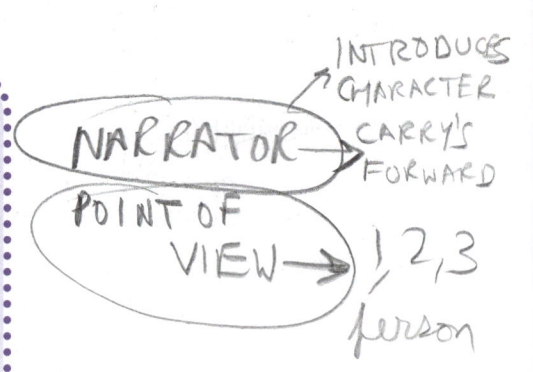

Developing your language – writing a story from the main character's point of view

1. The only person in this extract is Gregor. Find a sentence in quotation marks. Why does the author use quotation marks if Gregor is not talking to anyone?

2. The author describes Gregor's room and the weather. Why do you think the author includes this information?

3. Gregor 'found himself transformed into some kind of monstrous vermin'. Find another way to say the opening sentence to grab your reader's attention. Do not use an exclamation mark.

Word builder

1. The author describes Gregor's new size and shape, with an 'armour-like back'. Make a list of words and phrases the author uses to describe Gregor's beetle body.

2. Make a list of words and phrases that describe the movement of Gregor's 'jittery' legs. Do these words suggest that Gregor has much control over his legs' movements?

3. The title of Kafka's story is *Metamorphosis*. Use a dictionary and explain in your own words why Kafka may have chosen this title.

Key concept

Semi-colon

The semi-colon (;) allows a writer to join two or more sentences on the same subject into one sentence. It is used to:

- link phrases that are about the same thing or that complement each other in some way. **Example:**

    Throwing off the bedspread was quite simple; he needed only to puff himself up a little and it fell down of its own accord.

- to join two or more ideas that are of equal importance. **Example:**

    He would have needed arms and hands to raise himself; but instead of those, he had only these many little legs, which were continually fluttering about, and which he could not control anyhow.

- to separate items in a description or a list. **Example:**

    He pushed himself slowly on his back towards the bedpost so that he could lift his head more easily; he found the itching spot, which was covered with lots of little white dots he had no idea how to interpret.

Remember

A complex sentence has one main clause and one or more subordinate or dependent clauses. The main clause is the most important part of the sentence.

Using semi-colons in complex sentences

1. Look at the following sentence:

    Throwing off the bedspread was quite simple; he needed only to puff himself up a little and it fell down of its own accord.

    What does the second part of the sentence, after the semi-colon explain about the first half?

2. Look at Paragraph 4 from the *Metamorphosis* extract.
    a How many sentences are there?
    b Rewrite the paragraph using only simple and compound sentences.
    c Why did the author choose to use a semi-colon in a long complex sentence rather than shorter sentences?

Alternative reality

Lilliput

1 *Gulliver is shipwrecked, and swims for his life, gets safe on shore in the country of Lilliput, is made a prisoner,*
5 *and carried up the country.*

I lay down on the grass, which was very short and soft, where I slept sounder than ever I remember to
10 have done in my life, and as I reckoned, above nine hours; for when I awaked, it was just daylight. I attempted to rise, but was not able to **stir**: for as I happened to lie on my back, I found my arms and legs
15 were strongly fastened on each side to the ground; and my hair, which was long and thick, tied down in the same manner. I **likewise** felt several slender **ligatures** across my body, from my armpits to my thighs. I could only look upwards; the sun began to grow hot, and the light **offended** mine eyes. I heard a confused
20 noise about me, but in the **posture** I lay, could see nothing except the sky.

In a little time, I felt something alive moving on my left leg, which advancing gently forward over my breast, came almost up to my chin; when bending mine eyes downwards as much
25 as I could, I **perceived** it to be a human creature not six inches high, with a bow and arrow in his hands, and a **quiver** at his back. In the meantime, I felt at least forty more of the same kind (as I **conjectured**) following the first. I was in the utmost astonishment, and roared so loud, that they all ran back in a
30 fright; and some of them, as I was afterward told, were hurt with the falls they got by leaping from my sides upon the ground. However, they soon returned, and one of them, who ventured so far as to get a full sight of my face, lifting up his hands and eyes by way of admiration, cried out in a **shrill**, but distinct
35 voice, *Hekinah degul*: the others repeated the same words several times, but I then knew not what they meant. I lay all this while, as the reader may believe, in great uneasiness.

from *Gulliver's Travels* by Jonathan Swift

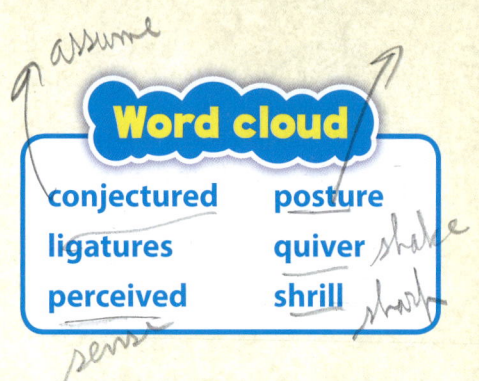

Word cloud
- conjectured
- posture
- ligatures
- quiver
- perceived
- shrill

Glossary

to stir to move

likewise similarly

offended to cause unpleasant feeling

Understanding

1. Gulliver swims ashore and finds a pleasant place to lie down and sleep. Why?
2. Why can't Gulliver move when he wakes up? Find a quotation in the extract to support your answer.
3. How does the author show the reader that the people of Lilliput are very small? Find words or phrases in the extract to support your answer.
4. Gulliver hears words in the language of Lilliput. Suggest a possible meaning for *Hekinah degul*. Use the context of the phrase to help you.
5. Look at how many times the author uses the first person 'I' in the opening paragraph. The author writes about what happens to Gulliver as if he is a real person telling his story. But this is a fictional first person. Why do you think Jonathan Swift chose to write in the first person *as if he is* Gulliver?

Remember

Archaic language is no longer in everyday use. It is old-fashioned. You can use the context in which it is written to work out what it means.

Word builder

Look at the words and phrases below and find a way to say them in modern English. Use a dictionary to help you.

1. 'attempted to rise'
2. 'but was not able to stir'
3. 'the light offended mine eyes'
4. 'in the posture I lay'
5. 'ventured so far as'

Alternative reality

Key concept

Embedded clauses

Embedded clauses are called **subordinate** or **dependent clauses** because they are part of a larger sentence but they are not the most important piece of information.

Example:

Fatima lost her bag.
Fatima's mother gave her the bag for her birthday.
Fatima lost it (the bag) on her way home.

We can join these sentences together using an embedded clause and an **adverbial**.

Fatima lost her bag, which her mother had given her on her birthday (*embedded clause*), on her way home (*adverbial phrase*).

Remember

A clause is part of a sentence which requires more information to create a full and proper sentence.

Using embedded clauses

Answer the following questions.

1. Here are the beginnings, middles, and ends of four mixed-up sentences with embedded clauses. Sort these and join the parts together to make longer sentences.

   You need to add a 'who' or 'which' to each sentence. You also need to put in the correct punctuation. **Example:**

   My uncle, who is very old-fashioned, doesn't have a television.

the elephants	have convincing characters	looked too human to me
my uncle	had been walking for hundreds of miles	keep me reading all night
the Hobbits in the movie	(who) is very old-fashioned	finally found water
the best sort of books	according to the author have furry feet	doesn't have a television

2. Write three sentences of your own with embedded clauses. Start your embedded clause with a 'which' or 'who' connective. Don't forget to use commas.

Adverbial phrases

Answer these questions.

1. What do the following adverbial phrases have in common?
   - As Gregor Samsa woke one morning from uneasy dreams . . .
   - In a little time, I felt something alive moving on my leg . . .
   - In the meantime, I felt at least forty more . . .

2. Write two short sentences with an adverbial that show *where* something is happening. Don't forget to put the comma after the adverbial phrase. **Example:**

   Lying back in bed, he decided not to get up.

3. Write two short sentences with an adverbial that show *how* something is happening. **Example:**

   Moving cautiously, hoping no one would hear him, he opened the door.

> **Remember**
> Adverbial phrases tell us when (time), where (place), and how (manner).

Practising your language skills

Answer the following questions about adverbials and embedded clauses.

1. Look at this paragraph with the adverbial phrases and embedded clauses underlined. Notice how adverbial phrases and embedded clauses all need commas.

   Make two lists: one for adverbial phrases and another for embedded clauses.

   Although it was getting dark, Bob, who didn't like the dark, knew he had to go out. It was his turn to lock the henhouse. The night before, a fox had been seen near the garden. The fox, which looked very thin, was obviously hungry. Trying to be quick so he could get the job done as fast as possible, Bob put on his jacket, which he had left by the door, and picked up the big torch.

2. Use the picture to the right to write a paragraph of your own. Include adverbial phrases and embedded *who/which* clauses.

3. When you have finished, swap paragraphs with a partner. Underline the adverbials and embedded phrases in your partner's writing and hand it back to see if you are right.

11

Alternative reality

🎧 Film adaptations

Melanie and Josh are discussing fantasy books and movies. Listen to their opinions.

Understanding

1. What sort of movies are Josh and Melanie discussing?
2. 'In the mind's eye' means *seeing something in your imagination*. How does this apply to fantasy books and films?
3. Melanie says 'If a director is making a film of a book he – or she – should respect what the author has written.' Find another way to say this in your own words.
4. Josh disagrees with Melanie when she says all fantasy stories are the same. Explain their different points of view.
5. Discuss whether you think some movies are better than the books they come from. Take turns to give your opinions and explain your reasons. After ten minutes, stop your conversation and write down the conclusions your group has come to. Share these ideas with your class.

💬 Working with register

Melanie and Josh are friends talking together. They use an *informal register*. That means they are speaking using colloquial expressions and interrupting each other. If they had been speaking with a teacher or an adult they did not know, they would have used a more *formal register* and been more polite about interrupting and disagreeing.

Role-play different people speaking about the same film and its special effects.

1. You are a university professor coming out of a fantasy movie with your colleague, who is also a professor. You did not enjoy the film.
2. You are with your friends. You thought the film was very good.
3. One of you is the professor; one of you is the student. Discuss your opinions of the film's special effects.

Glossary

I'll grant you that a way of saying 'Yes, all right'

awesome amazing

it wasn't remotely realistic not even near to being realistic

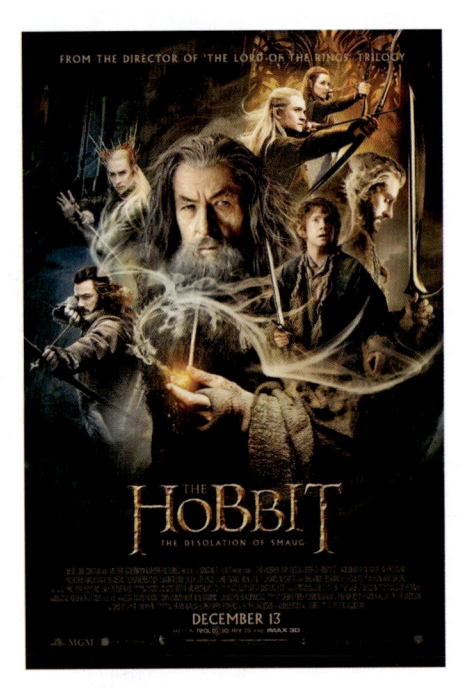

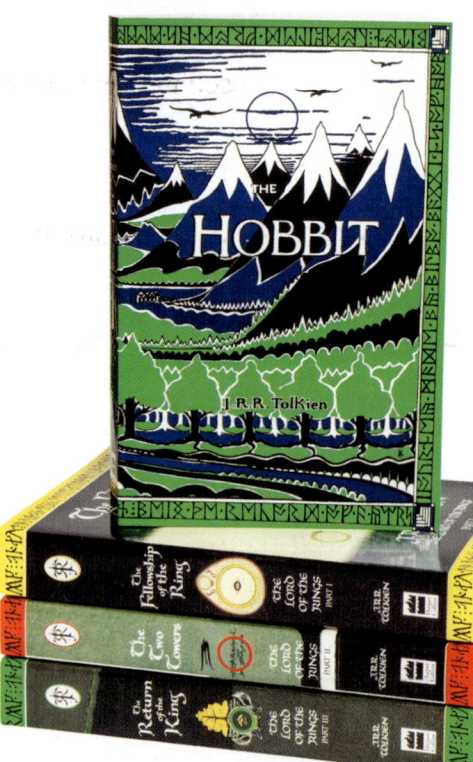

Making a film of a book

1. Think about a book that you have read that would make a good movie. It can be in any genre.

2. Decide with a partner which book you are going to turn into a film. One of you is the producer in charge of the business side of the film; one of you is the director in charge of what happens on the screen.

3. Write notes on:

   a *Why* this book would make a good film. Consider:
   - action
   - intrigue
   - special effects
   - length of the film
   - target audience
   - popularity of genre
   - publicity.

4. Write down *how* you will turn the story into a screenplay. Consider:
   - setting and location (where and when) – the same or different to book
   - actors who will play main characters
   - actors for secondary characters
   - whether costumes and make-up are for a particular period or to be created
   - what special effects are needed and why
   - what stunts the film will include, if any.

5. When you have finished, find out if anyone else has chosen the same book.

   a If so, compare your film version with theirs.

   or

   b If not, compare your film with an existing film in a similar genre.

Alternative reality

✏️ Writing a fantasy story

Fantasy stories involve imaginary beings in the real world or present the reader with an alternative reality. Characters may be real people or they may seem ordinary but have magic and/or supernatural powers. A good writer can turn a quite ordinary experience into something extra-ordinary.

Write a fantasy story that begins with two people waiting for something or someone to arrive. Think about the following:

- who is waiting
- what or who they are waiting for
- the setting – where it happens
- what happens to the character(s) at the end of the story.

Before you begin, decide whether you want to write in the *third person* about a fictional character, or if you want to write in the *first person* as if you are the main character.

Plan your story so it has a clear beginning, middle, and a surprising or satisfying end. Use the following flowchart to help you.

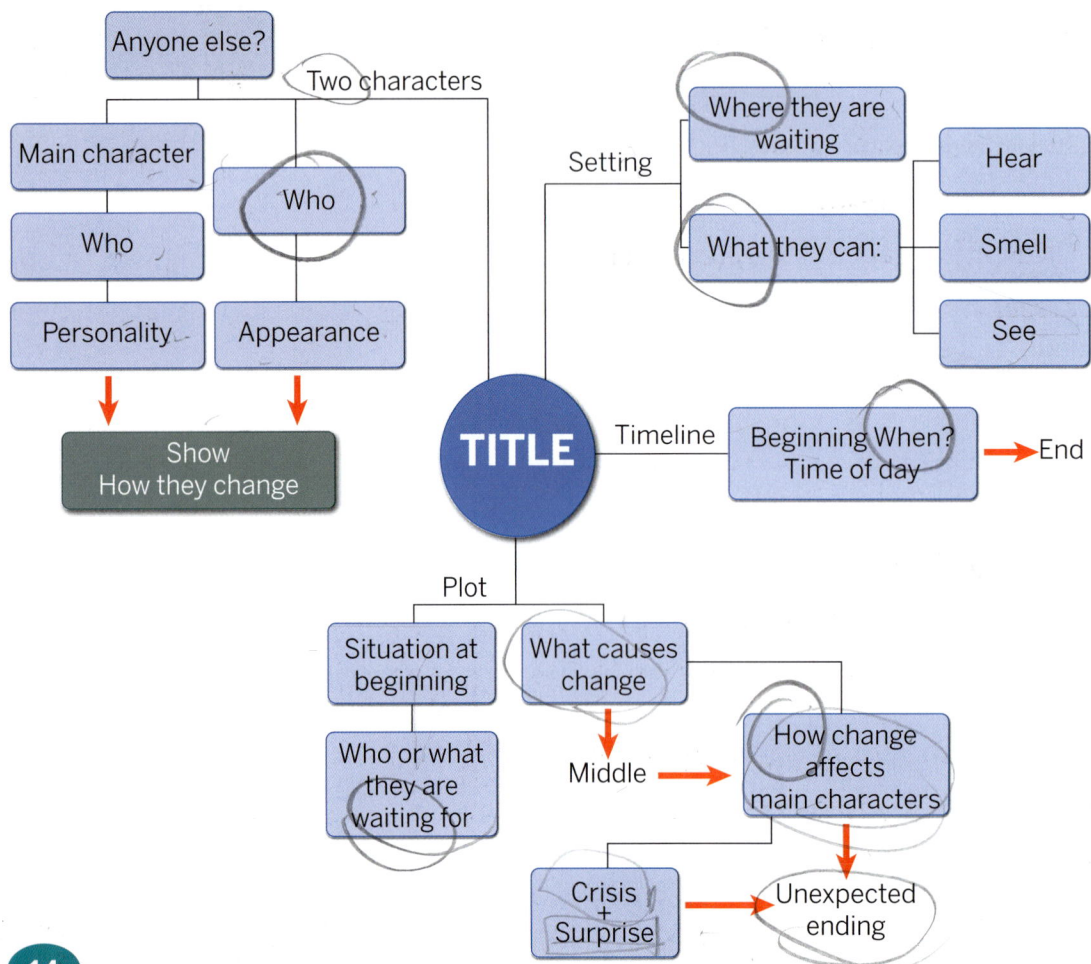

Characters:
- Anyone else?
- Two characters
- Main character → Who → Personality → Show How they change
- Who → Appearance → Show How they change

Setting:
- Where they are waiting → Hear
- What they can: → Smell, See

TITLE

Timeline: Beginning When? Time of day → End

Plot:
- Situation at beginning
- Who or what they are waiting for
- What causes change → Middle → How change affects main characters
- Crisis + Surprise → Unexpected ending

14

When you are happy about what is going to happen in your story, use the following template to plan your paragraphs. The reader should be surprised at the end, but you as the writer need to know where your story is going and how it is going to end *before* you start writing.

Title	*Suggests* what is going to happen but does not give the game away.
Beginning	*Shows* how the day or event starts and gives information about the main character.
Middle	*Shows* who or what arrives and how this brings about a change. Include the main character's thoughts and feelings.
End	*Shows* how this event affects the main character. Write an unexpected ending of how that character will never be the same again.

Proofreading and editing

When you have finished the story, read it through carefully. Check that:

- you have achieved what you planned to do
- your writing is legible (easy to read)
- you have used a variety of sentences for different effects
- your spelling is correct
- your punctuation is correct.

Key concept

Writing a good story
- A good writer *shows* rather than tells.
- A convincing character has weaknesses or flaws.
- The main character changes in some way in the course of a story.
- Different types of sentences are used for different effects.
- Good stories rarely end with 'and then I woke up' or 'it was all a dream'.

Alternative reality

Spotlight on writing

Analysing the question

Before answering a writing question, before you even start planning, go back and look at the instructions carefully. Check:

- the style of writing (fiction or non-fiction) required
- if there is a specific audience *kids, adults, youth*
- if it is a story, whether it is the beginning, the whole story, or the end
- that you understand all the information given in the question.

Keywords

Write a short story where an ordinary event turns into something the reader does not expect.

Consider:

- what ordinary event is taking place
- who is involved
- how the setting and/or the characters are changed by what happens.

The keywords tell you how to answer the question. There are different ways to *keyword* a question. **Example:**

| WHAT I must write – complete story (not just the beginning or the end) | WHAT happens in the story – an ordinary event – WHERE? WHEN? |

Write a short story, where an ordinary event turns into something the reader does not expect.

| WHY it happens, and the result of the change | HOW it changes – the day, the place, and the characters |

When you have finished analysing the question, you can start planning. Keep going back to the question to ensure you are doing what you have been asked.

Have a look at this *wh–* plan to help you answer this type of question.

Planning – the *wh–* planning method

In a six-point *wh–* plan you decide:

| Who? | Where? | When? | Why? | What? | How? |

You do not have to follow a particular order but you do need to use each word.

- **Who** are your characters?
- **Where** are they?
- **When** does the story take place?
- **Why** does the strange event occur?
- **What** happens *before and after* the strange event?
- **How** does the main character change during the story?

When your plan matches the question, shows *what* happens and *how* it affects the main character, you are ready to write the story.

Answer this question using the advice above.

Aim to write one page in 30 minutes. Remember that you need to leave time to check spelling and punctuation.

Alternative reality

Evaluating

Here are two sample answers to this question. Read both stories.
Carry out the following tasks.

1. Read each story and think about:
   - how it matches the question
   - how it shows something unexpected
   - how the main character changes
   - whether it contains errors in spelling, punctuation or grammar
   - the overall effect of the story – is it convincing, funny, clever, sad, different?

2. When you have read the stories think about the content of each one (plot and characters) and decide which one is better. Explain your answer.

3. Look at the technical accuracy of each story and explain which is better.

4. Which story has the better content *and* the better, correct use of English?

Story 1 – The School under the sea

1   I rolled over in bed and slammed my hand down on the alarm botton. Seven o'clock time to get up. Time for school. Another boaring day of lessons and same old same old teachers. Nothing ever changes at my school nothing ever changes in my life.

5   At nine o'clock I was sitting in Geography next to Shavi, my best friend. He opened the atlas when the teacher handed it to him and gasped. I looked to see why. Shavi had openned it at the page for our country, like the teacher told us to. But our country wasn't there. There was just a space. I starred at the page. We
10 were now under the sea.

Slowly I turned my head and looked out of the window. A fish swimmed by. After that there was a shark. I nuddged Shavi. Look I said. Look!

Shavi opened and closed his mouth exactly like the fish. I
15 pointed to the map on our desk. Look, I said again.

"What are you boys doing? shouted Mr Jones the geography teacher.

"Please sir, I think we're um under watter, sir." I said.

"Don't be ridicilous boy, said Mr Johns.

"Um sir look" said Shavi and he pointed to the window.

20 There was a huge octapus creeture looking in. I started to laugh because I could see a school of fish then stopped because Mr Joans doesn't like us laughing in his lessons.

Story 2 – The Cabin

1 The huge purple creature called a Purpon growled as it staggered towards us. I knew I should run but I didn't think I'd be able to escape. Our planet has been taken over
5 by Purpons and Yellons. Yellons are yellow and dangerous, but not as big or strong as Purpons. My friend Tomias said, 'We'd better get out of here.' This was no way to start the day. We started to race across the
10 land where our garden used to be before the Purpons and Yellons started their war. I was in a panic but Tomias was calm. 'Let's get back to the cabin,' he said to me.

Our cabin wasn't far away but it was like
15 hours before we got back inside. Tomias banged our code on the door and Freda let us in. We have to have a code to keep the other kids out because our cabin is really small. It used to be my grandad's garden shed.

Freda looked at us. 'What's happened now?' she asked. Her voice
20 was like a scream. Freda is older than us. She's my sister and sort of behaves like she needs to look after us.

'There's a Purpon – it's coming this way.' Tomias said.

I went to sit on my blanket and tried to get my breath back. I didn't want to think about what would happen if the Purpon
25 found us. We'd be captured or something worst. There weren't many kids left anymore and the Purpons kept getting bigger. You didn't need to be a genius to figure out where the kids were going.

Suddenly the cabin started to shake. The door rattled. Freda screamed. Tomias jumped on his blanket bed and pulled a
30 blanket over his head. The door rattled again then it opened wide and a grey haired head looked in. 'Are you playing in here again?' Grandad said.

2 Dramatic discoveries

Explore
- the distant past of Argentina
- prehistoric caves in Spain and France

Create
- a drama script
- a blog article about a recent discovery

Engage
- in a discussion about science and history
- in a discussion about scary stories

Collaborate
- on inventing new words
- on understanding the personality of a character in a play

In this unit you will:

Reflect
- on how modern science is helping us to learn about and preserve the past
- on how Shakespeare created a villain

"Discovery consists of seeing what everybody has seen and thinking what nobody has thought."
Albert von Szent-Györgyi

Eureka!

Did you know the word *serendipity* comes from an old fairy tale, *The Three Princes of Serendip*, in which the characters constantly discovered things they were not seeking?

Thinking time

1. Do you think a scientist or historian sees things differently from other people?
2. Serendipity is finding something you didn't know you were looking for. Has this ever happened to you? Have any scientific discoveries been accidental?
3. Is there anything left to discover?

Speaking and listening

Read this passage about people who search for the past, then discuss their jobs.

Uncovering the past

Most inventions are improvements on previous ideas or items, and the world is constantly developing and changing, but knowing about the future depends on knowing about the past. For this we need historians and scientists, for example palaeontologists and archaeologists, who discover the past and solve ancient mysteries. Palaeontology is the study of the history of life on Earth as reflected in fossils in the Earth's crust. It involves physics, chemistry, biology, and geology. Palaeontologists look for clues to what happened in the very distant past to help us understand how the Earth has developed, and what may happen next.

Archaeology is the study of what remains of past civilisations. This involves examining geographical sites and ancient buildings to learn who lived there and how they lived. Archaeologists know about geography, geology, anthropology (the study of humans and their customs), and folklore.

Some of these scientists go on 'digs', seeking the answers to age-old mysteries that affect our current thinking and that could affect the future, such as: Why did dinosaurs become extinct? Could it happen to us?

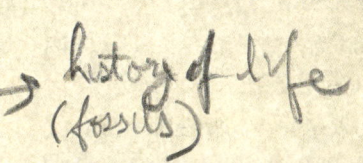

Work with a partner and answer the following questions:

1. Who studies the distant prehistoric past and who looks at the ruins of buildings?
2. One of you is a palaeontologist, the other an archaeologist. Make notes about your profession then tell your partner about it. Include: what you do, what you have studied and what you want to find.
3. Discuss how your jobs are similar and how they differ.

Dramatic discoveries

A spectacular discovery

This extract from a newspaper article describes finding a new type of dinosaur.

Battleship beast: colossal dinosaur skeleton found in southern Patagonia

By Ian Sample, Science Editor

1   **Dreadnoughtus schrani** unearthed in Argentina is most complete skeleton of plant-eating titanosaur recovered anywhere in world.

5   The spectacular remains of one of the largest beasts ever to walk the planet have been unearthed by fossil hunters in southern Patagonia.

The unique **haul** of bones includes a 10 metre-wide neck vertebra, a thigh bone that stands as tall as a man, and ribs the size of planks, representing the most complete skeleton of a colossal plant-eating titanosaur recovered anywhere in 15 the world.

The new species was so enormous that researchers named it Dreadnoughtus schrani after the dreadnought battleships of the early 20th century on the grounds 20 that it would fear nothing that crossed its path.

From measurements of the bones, scientists worked out that Dreadnoughtus reached 26 metres from snout to tail, making 25 it the largest land animal for which an accurate body mass can be calculated.

The colossal Dreadnoughtus lived around 77m years ago in a temperate forest at the southern tip of South America. Its 30 bodyweight equates to as many as a dozen African elephants or more than seven of the Tyrannosaurs rex species, according to Kenneth Lacorvara, a palaeontologist at Drexel University in Philadelphia. (…)

35 Lacorvara caught a first glimpse of the remains during a field trip to the **stunning** but barren **scrubland** of southern Patagonia in 2005. What appeared to be a small collection of bones soon became 40 an extensive haul of more than 100 bone fragments, exquisitely well preserved when the animal apparently drowned in quicksand.

Though staggering in its dimensions, close inspection of the bones revealed that the animal was not fully grown when it died. "That was a real shock to us," Lacorvara told the *Guardian* (...).

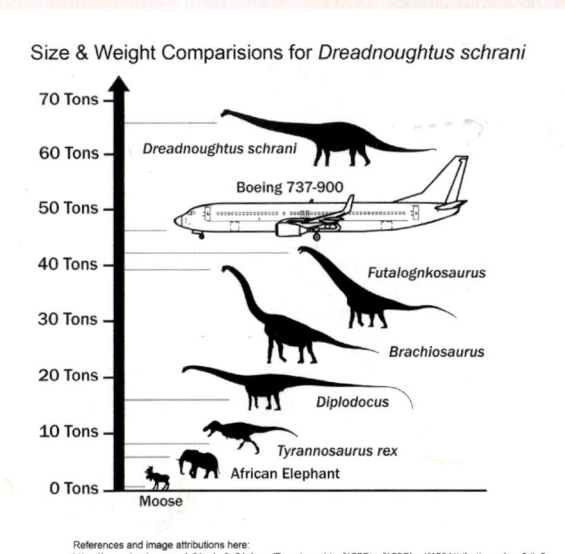

Relative sizes of the Dreadnoughtus schrani to other species. This animal was heavier than a Boeing 737

The site lies around 62 miles (100 km) off the power grid and four hours' drive from the nearest town. "I've spent a total of about a year living in my tent next to this dinosaur. We live very simply down there. We eat crackers for breakfast, a can of tuna and a piece of cheese for lunch, and every night we have a piece of meat on a stick," Lacorvara said. "Every couple of weeks we make a **foray** into town for food and showers."

In the late Cretaceous period, the site was a mixed forest of conifers and broad-leafed trees cut through by **meandering** waterways. The rivers were **prone** to flooding, and the sudden surge of water would have turned surrounding flood plains into sinking sand. The Dreadnoughtus was apparently in the wrong place at the wrong time. "Shortly after these individuals died, or as they died, they were buried quickly and deeply in what was essentially quicksand. That led to the high number of bones and the **exquisite** preservation," Lacorvara said. (...)

From an article in the UK newspaper, the *Guardian*, 4 July 2014

Word cloud

exquisite   prone
foray   scrubland
haul (n)   stunning
meandering

Dramatic discoveries

Understanding

Answer the following questions using information from the article.

1. a What name has been given to the dinosaur? *dreadnoughtus s.*
    b Why was it given this name? *largest ship*
    c What type of dinosaur is it? *herbivore*
2. Explain in your own words how the titanosaur may have died, then find a quotation in the article (words or a phrase) to support your answer. → *sinking into quicksand*
3. How does the area where the skeleton was found differ from how it used to be when the dinosaur lived there? Find words and phrases in the article to support your answer. *barren vs conifer trees*
4. How does the writer try to help the reader understand how big the titanosaur is? Give two examples from the article. *comparing to elephants, t-rex*
5. What sort of life has the palaeontologist led during the dig? Think about the location of the dig and how this affected Lacorvara's lifestyle. → *animal*

Word builder

Writing a diary entry

Imagine it is the day on which the 100th bone has been found. You are a palaeontology student who has been working on the dig. Describe your feelings as you realise there are now enough bones to recreate the vast skeleton of the titanosaur. Write your thoughts in your diary. Use at least 5 words from the Word cloud. Start with the word *Eureka!*

Include:
- what life on the dig in Patagonia has been like
- something about your daily routine
- the moment you realise that your team has found the 100th bone
- what finding this bone means.

Key concept

Direct and reported speech

Direct speech uses inverted commas. Reported speech does not have inverted commas and is often introduced by 'that'.

Direct speech: "The size of the beast was a complete surprise," Jose Esquina, a history student, told us.

Reported speech: Jose Esquina, a history student, told us that the size of the beast was a complete surprise.

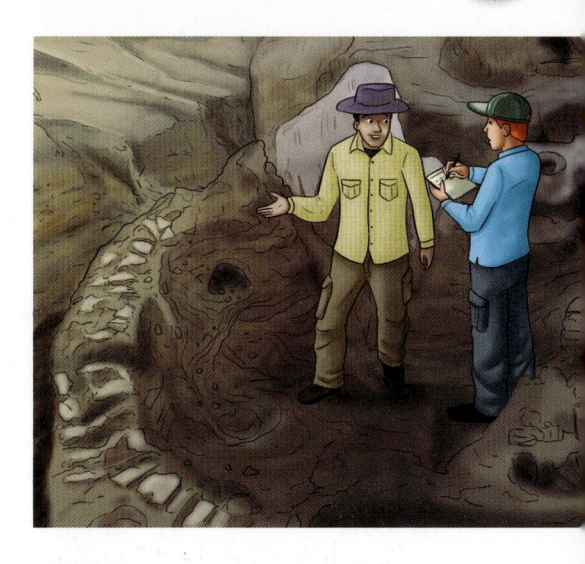

Developing your language – direct and reported speech

Although the dimensions of the dinosaur were staggering, close inspection of the bones revealed that the animal was not fully grown when it died. "That was a real shock to us," Lacorvara told the *Guardian* newspaper's reporter.

You are a journalist reporting on the discovery. Rewrite the paragraph in your own words, using reported speech.

Writing a conversation

1. Write a conversation between Monica and Hanni about the discovery of *Dreadnaughtus schrani*. Monica thinks it is fascinating; Hanni thinks it is a waste of time and money. Include where the discovery was made and who made it.

2. Write a paragraph reporting on what Hanni said in the conversation. Start like this: *Hanni believes searching for the past is a waste of time. He said . . .*

Word builder

How many words do you know to describe something enormous?

1. Make a list of ways to say something is very big.
2. Use a dictionary to find the meaning and origin of 'colossal'.
3. The adjective 'titanic' also means huge. Who or what was a Titan?

Looking closely

Using language that is easy to understand

The article about *Dreadnoughtus schrani*, is written for a daily newspaper. Though this important and exciting discovery was made by highly qualified scientists the language of the article is easy to understand. It uses familiar comparisons to help us imagine the creature's colossal size.

Dramatic discoveries

💬 A dreadful discovery

Read the following scenes based on 'The Canterville Ghost', by Oscar Wilde. Examine how Wilde uses comedy.

1   **Scene 1** *Lord Canterville is selling his ancestral family home to an American, Mr Otis, whose family immediately moves in.*

    Lord Canterville: I ought to tell you, we haven't actually wanted to live here since my great-grandaunt … felt the
5   skeleton hands of Sir Simon on her shoulders.

    Mr Otis: My Lord, I am happy to pay for all furniture and fittings – including your family ghost – if he exists.

    Lord Canterville: Oh he exists, sir! Be warned! And he always
10 appears before a death in the family.

    Mr Otis: So does a doctor, Lord Canterville. I come from a modern country where we have everything money can buy. Believe me, if there were such a thing as a ghost, we'd have
15 one. Do you expect me to pay more for the pleasure of having a ghost on the premises?

    Lord Canterville: No, good heavens, no! Well, if you don't mind taking on Sir Simon, I'm happy to conclude the sale. But please remember, I did warn you.

20 Mr Otis: I understand, sir. However, there is no such thing as a ghost, and *if* Sir Simon *is* here, I will be forced to charge him rent.

    Scene 2 *Sir Simon, in a white sheet, looks at a pot of cleaning fluid and a paint box left open on a table. His portrait is on the floor and the*
25 *bloodstain has gone from the rug.*

    Sir Simon: Who do these people think they are? They walk in here like they own the place, leave their possessions wherever they like and… remove my portrait *[puts it back on the wall]*…
30 *and* remove my bloodstain. And that's just their first day! I've kept this bloodstain here for 300 years … and I'm certainly not going to let a few Americans ruin it – or my ghostly reputation – now. These people must go!
35 *[Lets out a terrifying moan and disappears].*

Glossary

furniture and fittings everything in the house, including rugs and curtains

dock his wages deduct money for breaking the coffee cup

Scene 3 *Next morning at breakfast.*

Washington Otis [son]: Everyone sleep well last night? Oh, look, the bloodstain is back. I guess there is a ghost after all.

Virginia Otis [daughter] opens her paint box.

Virginia Otis: That's odd; my brick red paint has all gone.

James, the butler, enters with a tray of coffee and cups.

Mrs Otis: Look, the portrait of that horrid Sir Simon fellow is back on my wall! James, did you do that?

James: The portrait *[drops tray]*… agh! *[faints]*

Washington: Oh dear, the butler has fainted. Remember to dock his wages, Mother.

Understanding

Answer the following questions.

1. Why is Sir Simon angry with the Otis family? Give two reasons.
2. What is Mr Otis's attitude to hearing about Sir Simon? Give two examples and find quotations to support your answer.
3. What do you think has happened to the brick red paint?

Continuing the scary scenes

Sir Simon reappears late the next night. A tremendous crash brings everyone rushing downstairs to discover an old suit of armour has fallen and Sir Simon is sitting rubbing his knees. He then walks through the family and disappears. Mr Otis's sons decide to trap Sir Simon.

Write another scene with Sir Simon and the sons, describing their plan to trap Sir Simon.

1. Write your scene in the form of a play script.
2. Acts out your play script in groups.
3. Compare the different ways that have been found to trap the ghost.

Dramatic discoveries

Combining words

Making old words into new words

We often put two words together to create a new meaning, for example: *fossil* + *hunter* = someone who hunts for fossils.

We do this for new ideas and inventions. For example: *skate* + *board* = *skateboard*

Look at the words below, which are all associated with modern sports. How many words can you make by mixing and matching words from each of the two boxes? Write a list. You can use each word more than once.

The first one has been done for you: *windsurfer*.

| wind roller skate ice snow kite | | hockey surfer blade rink skate board |

New words – portmanteau words

The term *portmanteau word* comes from Lewis Carroll's *Through the Looking Glass*, when Humpty Dumpty explains to Alice, "You see it's like a portmanteau — there are two meanings packed up into one word."

A portmanteau is a suitcase that has two separate sections. The picture illustrates how we make new words for new ideas, inventions or discoveries using words we already know.

titan + dinosaur = titanosaur
fog + smoke = smog
breakfast + lunch = brunch

Answer the following questions.

1. Join the two words together to make a portmanteau word:

   a *web + log* = blog
   b *parachute + trooper* = Para troope
   c *guess + estimate* = guesstimate
   d *helicopter + ski* = heliski

2. Work with a partner to invent some portmanteau words of your own for the following categories:
   - sport
   - entertainment
   - school
   - food
   - transport.

Prepositions

Little words that do a lot

Prepositions give us information about time and place.

The lighthouse keeper sat **in** his chair **throughout** the night, staring **at** the sky **through** his small window.

🔍 Looking closely

Sometimes we use a hyphen when we join two or more words together. Examples are *close-up*, *brother-in-law*, and *man-of-war* (a type of battleship). To make these nouns plural you sometimes need to change the first part: *brothers*-in-law, *men*-of war.

Key concept

Prepositions

Words that are prepositions can also act as adverbs, but a preposition requires an object and an adverb does not:

If you want to see the moonlight, go **outside**.   **outside** = adverb

There was a long queue **outside** the cinema.   **outside** = preposition

Prepositions usually come before nouns and noun phrases. For example:

The palaeontologists camped **beside** the dig.

The dreadnoughtus was **in** the wrong place **at** the wrong time.

Prepositional phrases

A prepositional phrase is made up of the preposition, its object, and associated adjectives or adverbs.

We use prepositional phrases for many purposes:
- as adverbials of time and place
- with a noun phrase
- to show who did something
- after certain verbs, nouns and adjectives.

Example:

The student, who was **in the library** looking **for information on fossils**, was looking **through an old journal** the librarian had found **in a box under his desk**.

Answer the following questions.

1. Write a sentence about where you are now and underline the prepositions and/or prepositional phrase.
2. Write two sentences about what you did last weekend and ask a partner to find the prepositions and/or prepositional phrases.
3. Write a short paragraph about finding something surprising in your grandmother's cupboard. Include as many prepositions and prepositional phrases as you can.

29

Dramatic discoveries

The king under the car park

Read this blog post about finding the skeleton of Richard III, an English king, under a car park. Then listen to a radio news broadcast about it.

Discuss how the discovery affects what people know about a king who is supposed to have murdered his nephews and who died in battle in 1485.

The skeleton identified as King Richard III

🌐 http://www.plantagenethistory.blogspot.com

The king under the car park

I've been reading about the discovery of the much-hated (or misunderstood) King Richard III. His skeleton was located under a car park in Leicestershire, England. Richard III, a **Plantagenet**, was the last monarch of the House of York, and the last English king to die in battle.

The skeleton, with a slightly curved spine, has now been examined and scientists have proved its identity through DNA analysis of a 17th-generation Plantagenet descendent. It is fascinating, the power of modern science to play historical detective. But what I'd like to know is: did Richard really murder his young nephews in the Tower of London?

In his play *Richard III*, Shakespeare created a hideous, horrible villain that people actually believe in. But as far as I know, when Edward IV died in April 1483 (a hundred years before Shakespeare's play) Richard *did* escort his nephew, 12-year-old Edward V to the Tower of London, where he was joined by his little brother, and the two young princes never appeared again. At the time, it was rumoured they'd been murdered by Richard so he could be king. So Shakespeare's version could be true.

Glossary

carbon dated when organic objects have been dated using measurements of the amount of radio carbon they contain

historical sources original documents and evidence from the period

osteo-archaeologist an archaeologist specialising in bones

Plantagenet a ruling English family of the House of York

potentially fatal capable of killing

rigorous study a careful and thorough examination

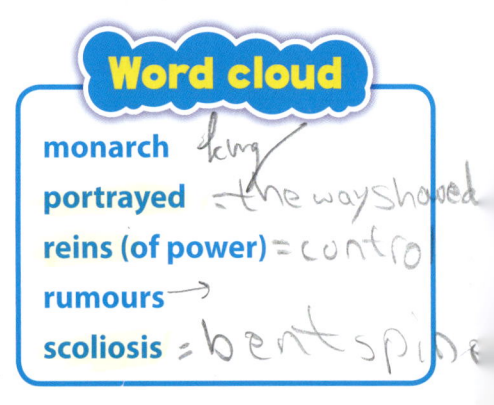

Word cloud

monarch
portrayed
reins (of power)
rumours
scoliosis

Understanding

Answer the following questions.

1. Who was the real Richard III? *last king of house York*
2. What does the discovery prove about how Shakespeare portrayed the King?
3. How has modern science been used to identify the skeleton found in Leicester? *DNA analysis of 17th generation*
4. The archaeologist Richard Buckley said the bones had been subjected to a *rigorous study*. Why do you think it was so important to study the skeleton?
5. Why, in your opinion, do historians need to look at historical sources again in this case? *verify facts*

Word builder

1. Match the words and expressions from the Word cloud with their meanings.

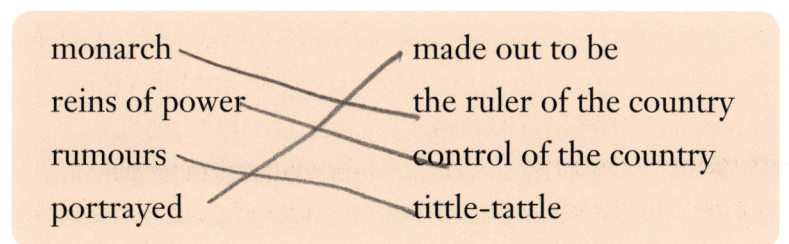

monarch	made out to be
reins of power	the ruler of the country
rumours	control of the country
portrayed	tittle-tattle

A portrait of Richard III

2. Why do you think the people who wrote the news about the discovery of the king's skeleton used the words in the Word cloud and not the other words and expressions?
3. Use information from the blog and the news broadcast to write a paragraph on the discovery for an international newspaper. Use words and expressions from the glossary and Word cloud. Write in a formal, informative style. → *facts, small sentences, simple words*
4. When you have finished, ask a partner to read it out in a formal style.

Dramatic discoveries

✏️ Writing a summary – a good night's sleep

Read this blog article about getting enough sleep.

http://www.teenagehealth.blogspot.com

What time is bedtime?

1 Lately, I've been getting worried about our twins' bedtime and lack of sleep. It's common knowledge that most teenagers don't get enough sleep. Gloria, who has a
5 wide social network, is in constant contact with her friends; Tobias is a grade A achiever and has to stay top of the class. So in one way or another, these two kids are just too busy to sleep. But they need sleep, especially
10 as the one thing they have in common is playing competition-level tennis.

   As a doctor, I know that not getting enough sleep can build into a serious sleep deficit. Teenagers with a sleep deficit find
15 it hard to concentrate or do any form of academic work effectively. They can also have emotional problems, and it seriously affects sports performance.

   Research shows that adolescents need
20 about nine hours' sleep a night. That means, ideally, a teenager who wakes up to prepare for school at 7 a.m. should go to bed around ten o'clock at night. Studies show, however, that many teens have trouble falling asleep
25 that early. It's not because they don't want to sleep; it's because their brains are working later in the evening and they simply aren't ready for bed. During adolescence, the body's biological clock is reset, telling a teenager to fall asleep
30 later at night and wake up later in the morning than they did when they were younger.

   As a sports' doctor, I also know most young athletes live for their sport. In addition to healthy eating, they need to think about healthy sleeping. Sleep plays a major role in 35 athletic performance and competition results. The quality and amount of sleep athletes get is often *the key* to winning. If sleep is cut short, the body doesn't have time to rest, create memory, and release hormones. A study in 40 the journal *SLEEP* confirms the role of a good night's slumber in athletics and team sports. There is a serious decline in split-second decision making following a poor night's sleep, which could be catastrophic for individual or 45 tennis singles or team players alike. Results also show increased accuracy in well-rested subjects. Good hydration and the right diet are only part of training and recovery. Good sleep is vital to prevent the possibility of fatigue, low 50 energy, and poor focus at game time. It may also help recovery after the game.

Understanding

Imagine you are doing a school project on sleep and sport.
Use the blog post opposite to help you answer the following questions.

1. Why do teenagers not feel sleepy early in the evening?
2. How does sleep affect sports performance?

Glossary

hydration drinking enough water

sleep deficit the number of hours needed to catch up on sleep

slumber peaceful sleep

Writing a summary

Write a summary of up to 100 words of why a good night's sleep is important for success in sports performance. Before you start your summary, look at the plan below to help you.

Preparing for summary questions

Find key words in the question. Ask: Do I need all the information in the text or just some of it?

Read the text again carefully and identify the relevant phrases, sentences or paragraph(s) for your summary.

Look at the question again. Check that you are not including unnecessary details.

Write your summary, in your own words as far as possible.

Count the words and make changes if necessary.

Proofread your final summary and correct any spelling and/or punctuation mistakes.

Dramatic discoveries

Reading non-fiction

To answer this type of question you need to look at how two texts have been written.

- Look at each writer's style.
- Look at each writer's choice of words.
- Think about the audience each text is written for.

Here are two extracts about the discovery of prehistoric cave paintings and how modern science is helping to preserve them.

Text A

This is an extract from 'Barbara's blog'.

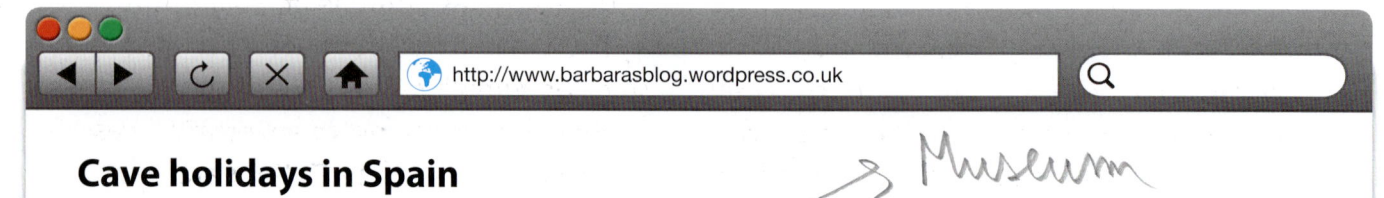

http://www.barbarasblog.wordpress.co.uk

Cave holidays in Spain

1 This summer I've been in two caves in Northern Spain looking at prehistoric artwork.

El Castillo Cave

5 The paintings on the walls of El Castillo Cave have been dated at more than 40 000 years old. It contains what might be the oldest cave art in the world! …Some scientists think the paintings were done by
10 Neanderthals.

As you walk through the cave, you see rows of red hand-prints and patterns of dots on the walls. There are also really detailed drawings of animals, including horses, deer,
15 bison, goats, mammoths, and dogs. What impressed me most were the hand-prints. They look small – smaller than mine, that is. Obviously we weren't allowed to touch the paintings but I waved one of my hands
20 in front of the low light from the torches to compare. Perhaps the prints were done by young children.

Altamira Cave → Museum

In Altamira Cave, there are images of bison that show whoever painted them had very
25 impressive art skills because they used the shape of the cave walls, the curves and contours, to make the bison appear three-dimensional. You can almost see them moving; galloping across the hills. There
30 are also depictions of goats, horses, female deer, and wild boar, as well as some abstract shapes, red spots, and hand prints. This cave is not actually open to the public, but we explored an amazing replica at the Altamira
35 Museum. Not the same as the real thing in El Castillo, though…

40 000

Text B

This is an extract from an article about the discovery of a prehistoric cave in France.

France recreates prehistoric paintings from Chauvet Cave

1   (…) Jean-Marie Chauvet noticed air whistling out from a crack on a plateau in southern France, so he and fellow cave enthusiasts went to investigate. What they
5   found that Sunday in 1994 still fills Chauvet's voice with wonder: an immense cave covered with prehistoric paintings of horses, mammoths and rhinos – paintings so vivid, he says, it felt like the Stone Age artists had
10 just moments ago put down their ochre and walked away.

   The discovery of the long-hidden artwork created a sensation, but the site was quickly closed to the public. Just by breathing,
15 tourists could erode the images.

   Since most modern humans will never get to see the masterpieces in what is widely known as the Chauvet Cave, scientists, artists and the French government have
20 spent 56 million euros (about $60 million) and several years creating the next best thing: a near-exact replica of the cave about two kilometers (1.2 miles) away, including more than 400 paintings of horses, bears,
25 rhinoceros and mammoths, hand prints and carvings. Experts even recreated stalactites and stalagmites from the original site, as well as the cool temperatures and thick smell of humidity. (…)
30
   "What impressed us," Chauvet said, "was the freshness. (…) The paintings are as if they had just left, these men, these women" who painted them (…).

   It turned out they had been remarkably
35 well-preserved thanks to a rock fall about 23,000 years ago that concealed the site. The conditions kept the drawings in such a pristine state that some researchers doubted their authenticity.
40
   "This cave wasn't exposed to gusts of violent air," Chauvet said. "It was preserved, like in a jar."

www.ctvnews.ca

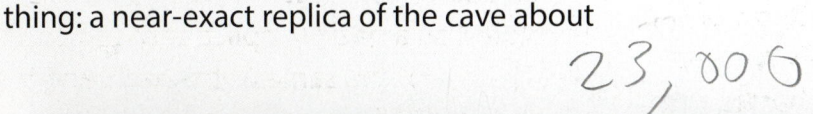

Dramatic discoveries

Understanding

Answer the following questions.

1. Which text is written in the most informal style and why?
2. Use Text A to answer the following questions.
   a Finish the following sentence, including a colon in your description.

   In El Castillo cave she saw... the oldest cave art in the world: these have been dated as ~~the~~ more than 60 000 years old

   b The writer says she liked one cave more than another. Which cave did she prefer? Explain why.
3. Use Text B to answer these questions about the discovery of Chauvet Cave in France.
   a How did Jean-Marie Chauvet find the cave?
   b What did the Stone Age artists paint?
   c How were the paintings preserved for so many years?
4. Write a 50-word summary describing what visitors can see in the replica of Chauvet Cave.

Sample answers

Read these three summaries which are sample answers to Question 4.

A In the Chauvet cave replica visitors can see: painted animals and handprints from the cave walls. There are four hundred paints of animals. They have copied the animals that are dead now like the mamoth. They have also made stalatights and stalamites and it's got the same temeperature and smell.

— Past participle —   ;
— Adverbial —   :
— Propositional —   conjuctions

36

B The replica of Chauvet Cave shows four hundred paintings copied from the real cave. that was like an art-gallery. Visitors get the experience as if they are in a real cave even if it's a replica. Scientists made the same atmosphere. ✗

C In the Chauvet Cave reproduction visitors can see and feel what it was like in the real prehistoric cave. There are over four hundred painted animals, carvings, and handprints. The replica has also got stalagmites and tites and the same sort of atmosfere as the real cave; damp humidity.

Using these bullet points to help you, discuss which summary you think is best. Explain your answer.

- The answer does not repeat words or phrases unless necessary.
- The answer is not over the word limit.
- The sentences flow together well.
- The answer contains the relevant information.
- The answer does not contain irrelevant information.
- The summary is mostly written in the writer's own words.
- The spelling is correct.
- There are only minor spelling mistakes.
- The grammar and punctuation are correct.

Compare your answer with the best of the three sample answers. Think about how your answer is as good as or better than this one. If it is not as good as you would like, make changes and write it out again.

— own words
— word limit
— no repetition
— only relevant
— spelling
— grammar & punctuation

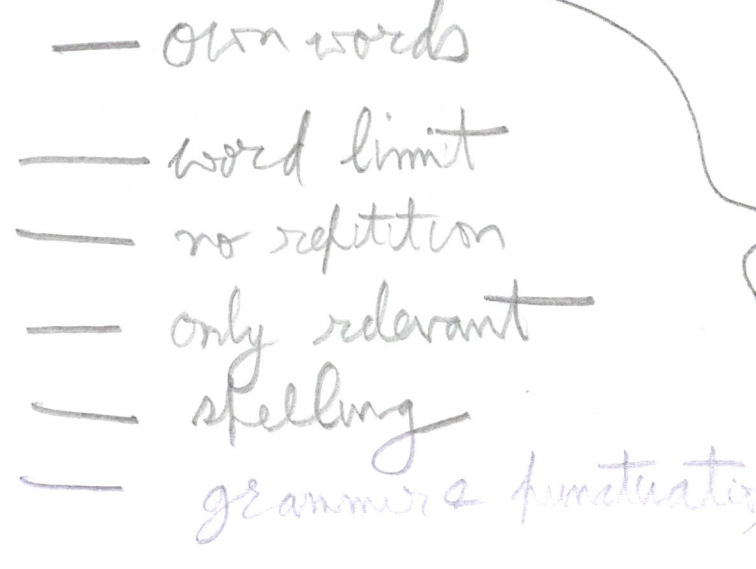

Summary

3 Fame

Explore
- Ancient Greece
- Ancient Turkey

Create
- A biographical profile
- A rock or film star

Engage
- In understanding different points of view
- In deciding what is the 'X factor'

Collaborate
- On writing a script
- In a group discussion

In this unit you will:

Reflect
- On what makes someone successful
- On what people think about beauty

"Handsome is as handsome does."

"Beauty lies in the eyes of the beholder."
Plato

"Success is falling nine times and getting up ten."
Jon Bon Jovi

Thinking time

1. 'Handsome is as handsome does.' People should be judged by what they do, not what they look like. Do you agree?
2. If beauty lies only 'in the eyes of the beholder', why are the mass media (newspapers and broadcasting) and social networks full of images of 'beautiful people'?
3. Jon Bon Jovi is an American singer-songwriter, record producer, philanthropist, and actor. His albums have sold over 130 million worldwide and he has been ranked at 50 on *Billboard* magazine's 'Power 100' (a ranking of 'The Most Powerful and Influential People In The Music Business') and was named by *People* magazine as one of the '50 Most Beautiful People In The World'. But what does the quote on the opposite page tell you about his personality and his success?

Speaking and listening

1. Look at the pictures of some very successful people. Work in pairs to try to put names to the pictures.
2. Decide which of the personality traits or qualities below helped them to achieve their success.
3. Which traits or qualities, if any, have *not* been used? Say why.

determination
self-confidence
passion
imagination
self-interest
vision
charisma
self-discipline

skill
talent
reliability
humility
persistence
single-mindedness
arrogance
moodiness

Fame

'The face that launch'd a thousand ships'

The Greek myth of Helen of Troy is thousands of years old, and has fame very much at its heart.

1 Tyndareus, King of Sparta, had a daughter, Helen, whose beauty was **renowned** throughout the isles of Greece and beyond. When time came for Helen to marry,
5 many chiefs and kings came to Sparta to beg for her hand. This put Tyndareus' kingdom in **jeopardy**. Helen could only choose one man, meaning those who were rejected might cause trouble. To avoid this,
10 Tyndareus insisted Helen's **suitors** agree to a 'suitors' oath': that they would come to the aid of whoever won her – should the need arise. Helen eventually chose Menelaus.

During this time, in Troy, also called
15 Ilium, three immortal goddesses decided the most handsome man on earth was Paris, Prince of Troy, and demanded he decide which of them was the loveliest. Paris, who had a keen eye for beauty, could not decide so, quietly, each of the divine
20 contestants offered him a bribe: Athena offered success in battle; Hera offered rule over Asia; Aphrodite promised him the most beautiful mortal woman as his wife. Paris, who some say knew all about Helen of Sparta, chose Aphrodite (and her bribe). Whether Paris knew Helen was now married or not, his eye for
25 beauty started the Trojan War.

Paris crossed the sea and became the guest of Helen and Menelaus, who had inherited the kingdom of Sparta. Shortly after, Menelaus left for Crete, and Helen was alone with their good-looking guest. The next we are told, Paris fled with Helen
30 and her priceless jewels back to Troy.

When Menelaus heard of the betrayal, he called in the 'suitors' oath', and raised a vast Greek army. Thousands of ships sailed for Troy to reclaim the lovely Helen.

Glossary
mortal a human being, rather than a god or immortal spirit

Word cloud
epic
jeopardy
renowned
suitors
superficial

40

The Trojan War lasted ten years and many
35 brave heroes died. Eventually, Menelaus
challenged Paris to a duel. Paris, whose
masculine beauty was greater than his skill
with arms, reluctantly agreed. But during their
combat, when Paris was at the point of death,
40 Aphrodite whisked him away in a cloud of dust.
Helen and Menelaus returned to Sparta and
lived happily ever after.

In Homer's **epic** poem 'The Iliad', Helen is
blamed for the terrible Trojan War, but by
45 modern standards she may not seem so wicked.
Selfish perhaps, but not the **superficial** person
she was accused of being. Nevertheless, Helen
will always be remembered in Christopher
Marlowe's words as having 'the face that
50 launch'd a thousand ships'.

The Trojan Horse, another tale of the Trojan War that you may enjoy learning about

Understanding

1. Why did so many chiefs and kings come to Sparta to beg for the hand of Tyndareus' daughter?
2. Who did Helen choose?
3. How did Tyndareus prevent the men Helen rejected from causing trouble?
4. Who were the three goddesses in Troy and what did they want from Paris?
5. Does this story suggest that the idea of beauty was responsible for the Trojan War? Explain your point of view.
6. This is a very ancient story. Work with a partner and re-write it for a modern audience.

Word builder

Helen's beauty was **renowned**, but people accused her of being **superficial**. The word 'superficial' comes from the Latin *superficies*, meaning 'surface'. How can this apply to someone's personality?

Fame

The Trojan War and epic verse

Christopher Marlowe (1564–1593) was an English playwright who translated Homer's epic poem about the Trojan War, 'The Iliad'. Homer recounts the siege of Troy, or Ilium, as it was known in ancient times. Marlowe also translated the work of Ovid, the Roman poet, who also included the story of Helen and Paris in his poems. Reading the Greek and Roman classics was part of a normal education in England at this time. Marlowe created these famous lines about Helen of Troy for a play called 'Dr Faustus'.

> 'Was this the face that launch'd a thousand ships,
>   And burnt the topless towers of Ilium?
>   (...)
>   O, thou art fairer than the evening air
>   Clad in the beauty of a thousand stars...'

Writing a personal account

Read what happened in the story of Helen of Troy again.

1. Working together, reflect on what the people involved may have thought and felt. Make notes on what made each of them act the way they did. Briefly say what each person did and, in your opinion, why. Be sure to include your observations on:
   - Tyndaraeus
   - Helen
   - Paris
   - Menelaus

2. Choose one of these characters: Helen, Paris, or Menelaus. Look again at what you thought about that person in the first part of this exercise. Consider how this person would speak and what tone of voice they had. Re-tell the story of the Trojan War from that person's point of view.

   Write in the first person (I), including:
   - your opinion of the other two people
   - your views on the ten-year war
   - how Helen and Menelaus were reunited.

Developing your language – describing someone's appearance

Using a thesaurus:

1. Make a list of at least five words to describe someone with a pleasant appearance.

2. *Handsome* and *good-looking* are adjectives that are often used to describe a boy or man with a pleasant appearance. Find at least two more.

3. *Elegant* and *pretty* are both positive ways to describe a girl or woman.

    a How and why do we use the words *elegant* and *pretty* in different ways?

    b Write a sentence for each word.

4. Look at the words below and decide what they all describe.

    a Put the words into categories. You need to decide what the categories are first.

    b Compare your categories with a partner. If you both have positive and negative categories, do you disagree on any words? If so, why?

crotchety   obstinate   gregarious   surly   compassionate
diligent   grumpy   honourable   vengeful   argumentative
fussy   moody   forthright   cheerful   frank   haughty

Speaking and listening – guess who!

Write two or three sentences to describe someone in the classroom but don't say who it is. Read your description aloud and see if the class can guess who it is. Be nice!

Philanthropy profile

Most people know Bill Gates **founded** the world's largest software business, Microsoft, with Paul Allen. Read the blog below to learn more of Bill Gates's story.

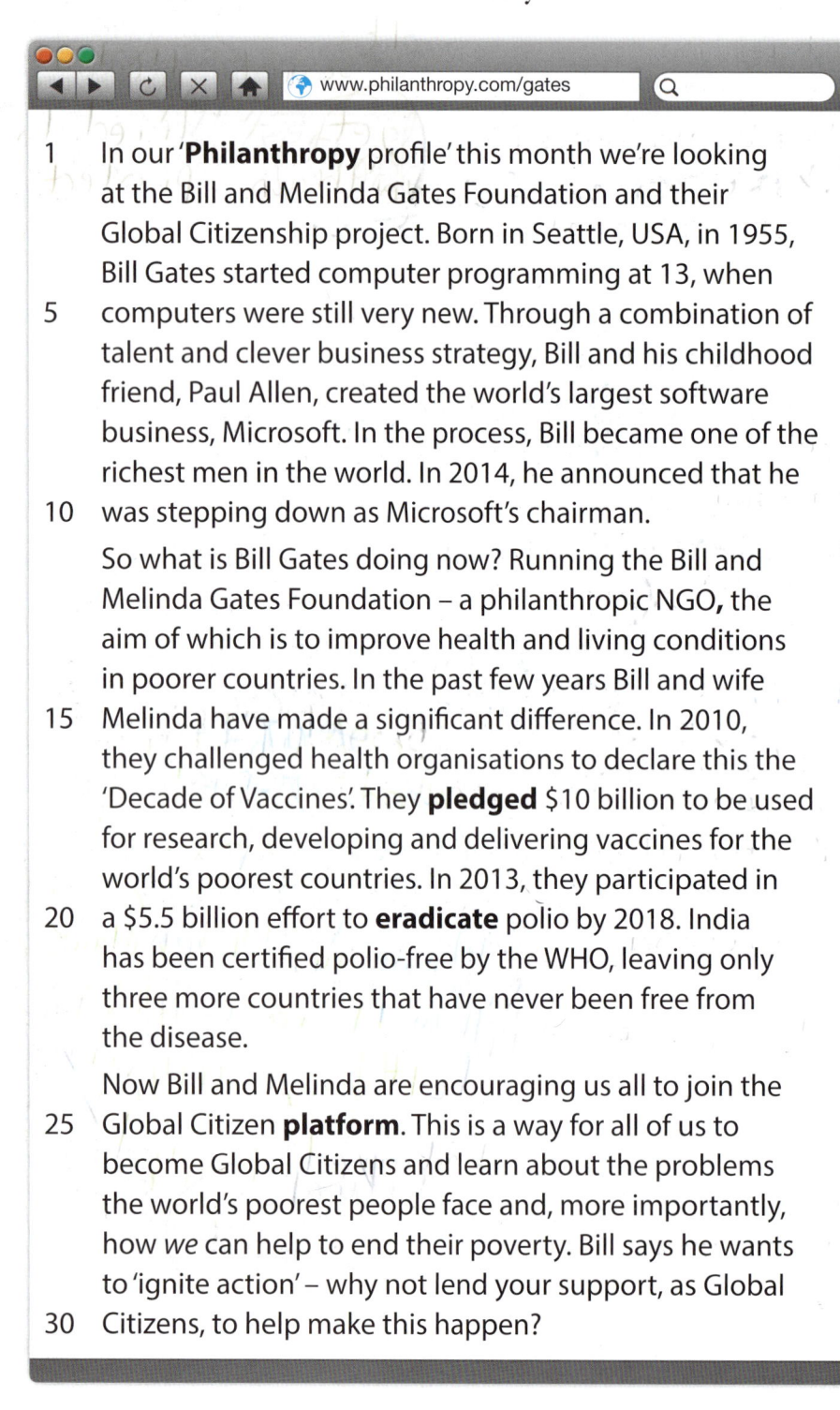

www.philanthropy.com/gates

1   In our '**Philanthropy** profile' this month we're looking at the Bill and Melinda Gates Foundation and their Global Citizenship project. Born in Seattle, USA, in 1955, Bill Gates started computer programming at 13, when
5   computers were still very new. Through a combination of talent and clever business strategy, Bill and his childhood friend, Paul Allen, created the world's largest software business, Microsoft. In the process, Bill became one of the richest men in the world. In 2014, he announced that he
10   was stepping down as Microsoft's chairman.

So what is Bill Gates doing now? Running the Bill and Melinda Gates Foundation – a philanthropic NGO, the aim of which is to improve health and living conditions in poorer countries. In the past few years Bill and wife
15   Melinda have made a significant difference. In 2010, they challenged health organisations to declare this the 'Decade of Vaccines'. They **pledged** $10 billion to be used for research, developing and delivering vaccines for the world's poorest countries. In 2013, they participated in
20   a $5.5 billion effort to **eradicate** polio by 2018. India has been certified polio-free by the WHO, leaving only three more countries that have never been free from the disease.

Now Bill and Melinda are encouraging us all to join the
25   Global Citizen **platform**. This is a way for all of us to become Global Citizens and learn about the problems the world's poorest people face and, more importantly, how *we* can help to end their poverty. Bill says he wants to 'ignite action' – why not lend your support, as Global
30   Citizens, to help make this happen?

Word cloud

eradicate
founded
philanthropy
platform
pledged

Glossary

NGO a non-governmental organisation
WHO World Health Organization

Understanding

1. Who founded the company Microsoft?
2. What is the purpose of the Bill and Melinda Gates Foundation?
3. How is the Gates Foundation helping health organisations around the world?
4. What is the aim of the Global Citizen platform?
5. What factors do you think contributed to Bill Gates's success with Microsoft and how might this influence his work with his charitable foundation?
6. Suggest ways Bill Gates can 'ignite action' to help eradicate poverty.
7. Write a formal letter to your principal suggesting your school gets involved with the Global Citizen platform. Include the following points:
   - What the Gates' NGO is doing
   - How school students can become involved
   - How this action will help both the charity and the students involved.

Word builder – philanthropy

1a Use a dictionary to look up the words *philanthropy* and *charity* and write down their meanings.
 b Is there a difference between philanthropy and charity? If so, explain what it is.
2. The noun 'platform' can be used in different ways. Give two examples.
3. Find another way to say 'a philanthropic platform'.

Writing a profile

Choose a person who is currently in the news, a business leader, a film star or sports personality and write a one page profile for a blog post. Include:
- how the person became well known
- what they have achieved
- what they are doing now
- why we ought to know about them.

Fame

Making adjectives
A -*tic* test

1. Working with a partner, make a list of all the words you know that end in -*tic*, such as *elastic* and *Atlantic*.

2. Divide the words into categories: nouns and adjectives. Some words can be both – look at the examples.

Nouns	Adjectives
elastic	elastic
plastic	plastic

3. Circle all the words you have written down that can be used to describe a person. For example:

   (Realistic)

Making adjectives

1. Write down the adjectives for the following nouns:
   - a charity
   - b philanthropy
   - c talent
   - d poverty — poor, impoverished
   - e wealth

2. Make verbs from these adjectives:
   - a decisive — To decide
   - b innovative — To innovate
   - c creative — To create
   - d critical — To critic, To critizise
   - e sympathetic — To sympathize

To test whether you have a verb, make its infinitive with the word 'to...'

Here is an example: **strong (adj)** = *to strengthen*

opinion — size — shape — age

The order of adjectives in descriptions

When we use two or more adjectives to describe a noun, we often put them in a certain order without thinking about it.

For example, we say:

- A pretty little flowery cup
- An expensive diamond bracelet
- An ugly old wooden chair

What do you notice about the second word in each of these examples?

We use an *opinion* word before one that is purely descriptive. The object being described comes last.

Arrange the following adjectives to describe the objects, then compare with a partner.

Noun	Adjectives				
A painting	French	priceless	impressionist		
A sports car	new	fantastic	Italian	red	
A band	noisy	amateur	dreadful	Norwegian	rock

The usual order for adjectives is:

opinion → size → shape → age → colour → nationality → material

So you could have:

An elegant, tall, narrow, nineteenth-century, red-roofed, Dutch, brick-built house.

A charming little, star-shaped, ancient, Sri-Lankan silver ring.

Working together, write as many adjectives as you can think of in the correct order for the following:

- A well-known monument or castle
- A famous painting or work of art
- A world-famous pop or film star
- A sports car or road-racing bike

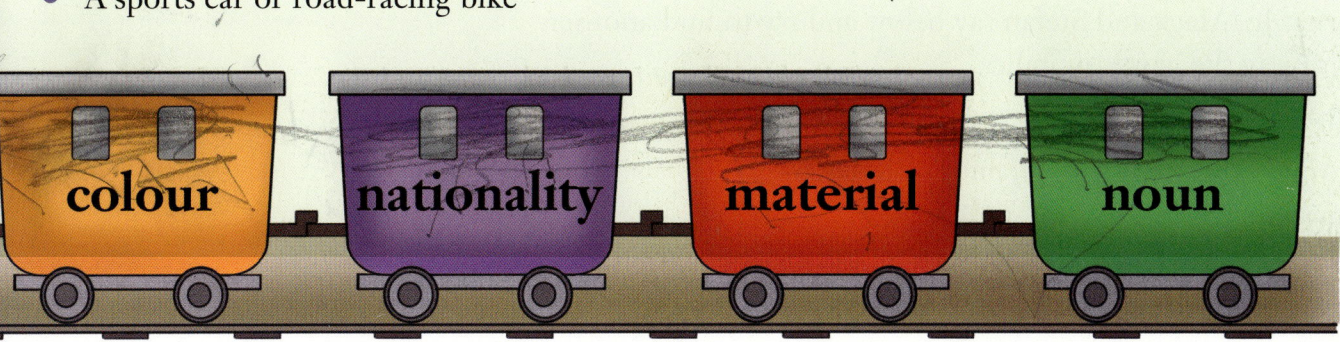

colour — **nationality** — **material** — **noun**

47

Fame

🎧 Charisma and star quality

Charisma is that special quality that makes somebody appear attractive or makes them **influential**. A charismatic person can be successful even if they aren't especially talented or good-looking. Listen to three people talking to a television chat show host about what makes some people famous.

You will hear: Gloria Gift, a pop singer; Mack Malloy, an actor; Stefan Astorius, a concert pianist. Their host is Jo Garcia.

Understanding

1. The guests on the show are all stage performers. What different talents are they famous for?
2. Do they think charisma is more to do with appearance or personality?
3. Do you think Mack's ability as a boy to 'clown about' helped him become successful?
4. Gloria says some backing singers 'don't want the limelight'. In your opinion, what might keep good singers at the back of the stage?
5. Explain in your own words what Stefan means by a 'dangerous aspect of charisma'.
6. Make notes on what makes the X factor or charisma, and add your own thoughts. You will be using these ideas later.

Developing your language – figures of speech

Being in the limelight is an expression or a figure of speech. We often use commonly recognised similes and metaphors in informal conversation as a quick way of saying something. Look at what Jo, Mack and Stefan say below and try to find another way to say the words in italics.

1. Jo: *let's get cracking*.
2. Mack: always *showing off* and *cracking jokes*.
3. Jo: You just *bounce onto the stage* and you've got the *audience eating out of your hand*.
4. Stefan: Luck can play a part in getting your first *lucky break*.

Word cloud

aspect	improvising
charisma	influential
devious	trait

Glossary

in the limelight at the front of the stage or the centre of attention. Before electricity, lime (calcium oxide) was heated to light up a stage.

💬 Speaking and listening

Talk about the following statements. Do you agree or disagree?

1. Charisma is the 'X factor'.
2. All performers – singers, actors and musicians – have got charisma.
3. Some people use their charisma to get what they want.
4. People don't always question why they think someone is 'wonderful'.
5. Charisma is something that can be achieved through practice.
6. It's only charisma that keeps famous performers and actors at the top.

Role-play – a star is born!

Imagine you are a talent scout. You are at a school concert and spot a boy or girl with genuine talent. You think you can make them successful and contact an agency.

In groups, decide which one of you is going to be the star, who is the talent scout and who are the agents.

Decide on the following:

- what name the new star should have
- what he or she should look like
- how he or she should play and/or sing to get into the music charts
- what he or she must do to be successful (should they go on tour all the time, make studio albums, be on television? What will get them noticed?)

Fame

✏️ Writing a television script

When you start to write a script, you need to plan the story-line carefully. Then you need to think about your characters. Decide who they are and how they develop and change during the course of the series, or standalone drama. Here are some guidelines to help you:

Structure

Most teleplays follow the three-act structure. **Act One** sets up the challenge your main character has to face. He or she has to encounter an obstacle and overcome it by the end of the play. Remember, the bigger the challenge, the greater the hero.

In **Act Two**, the character's mission becomes more complicated and the challenge more difficult. Other characters try to prevent the hero or heroine from succeeding. Consider introducing a **sub-plot**. By the end of Act Two your character is at a low point – about to lose, give up or worse, be eliminated.

In **Act Three**, your protagonist reaches a new level of determination and self-awareness. Having survived the worst, they still have to win. They look inside themselves and the viewer sees who they really are. Show them solving the problem, winning the day, defeating the enemy. End with a satisfactory 'feel-good' moment.

Dialogue

Before you start writing dialogue, decide exactly who your characters are. Create mini-biographies for them. Think about: age, education, family background, how they speak and show their emotions. Never write dialogue that doesn't move the story forward, and avoid long speeches. Break up dialogue with action or interjections from other characters. Always read the dialogue aloud to see if it sounds real.

> ⭐ **Tip**
>
> A **sub-plot** is a secondary story, usually introduced early in the second act, and brought to a satisfactory end before the exciting climax to your main story.

🔍 Looking closely

In a one-hour TV screenplay, Acts One and Three usually last about ten minutes, while Act Two lasts about 40 minutes. Professional script writers often use story boards to see how a story develops, and what is happening in each scene.

✏️ Writing

Below, you will see an advertisement for a new television detective series. It gives information about the main characters and what they do. Use these details to create memorable personalities and write **part of this exciting episode** for the series. Include stage directions for the actors and camera directions if you think they are necessary.

Your script should last a maximum of 15 minutes. Decide whether your scenes come at the beginning or end of the 40-minute episode.

Martin and Martina
Globetrotting private investigators
"No job too strange, no place too far."

Serious minded Martin and fashion-loving Martina (Tina) start the new series of a fascinating detective series in Amsterdam, hot on the trail of a priceless jewel said to have belonged to Helen of Troy. Their job is to find the jewel and take it to the British Museum for authentication. What Martin and Tina don't know is that there is a ruthless gang of treasure hunters after the jewel as well. Will Martin and Tina get the precious rock before the treasure hunters find it? Can they get it back to London safely? Watch the first exciting episode and find out.

Fame

💬 Speaking and listening

You are going to take part in a role-play discussion. This is a group activity which runs for about 10–15 minutes. There are four or five students in each group. Choose one of the topics below. When you have finished, watch each group's discussion and offer feedback on what they have done well, and where they can improve. Use the information on speaking and listening skills on page 54 to help you.

1. A chat show discussion about television crime series.

   In this option you take a role and discuss crime stories as that person. The discussion could include the following people:
   - a chat show host
   - actors who have played famous detectives such as Sherlock Holmes or Miss Marple
   - viewers who think crime on television encourages young people to think it is not serious or damaging to society.

   OR

2. You work for an advertising company. You have been asked to create an advertisement for a new type of bicycle specially designed for doing stunts. In your group discuss:
   - Who should be in the advertisement: a normal person or a famous young television or film actor?
   - What sort of stunt does the advertisement show?
   - Where does the stunt take place: on the street, in a residential area, someone's garden or a special venue?
   - Do you need to include safety factors in the advertisement?

> **Key concept**
>
> **Participating in a discussion**
>
> The main skills in this Speaking and listening activity are speaking in turn and responding appropriately. For this reason it is very important that no member of the group takes over the discussion or dominates the scene.

💬 Role-plays and discussions

You are now going to plan and carry out your own speaking and listening activity. Get together in pairs or groups and decide what you want to do, and how.

You may choose from:

a A role-play where each student plays the part of a member of a neighbourhood discussing a local problem (pair or group)

b Members of a family in a television series discussing something that matters to them (group)

c Discussing an issue such as hunting, or keeping dangerous animals as pets (group)

d Choosing the next actor to win an Oscar or prestigious award (pair or group).

Deciding what to talk about and how

- Gather ideas, making notes on what is said or suggested as you go along.
- Reduce the number of ideas to those that are most popular and practical.
- Choose a group leader to lead the discussion or direct the scene.
- Plan who is going to say what: who opposes each other; who agrees with whom.
- If you are doing a role-play, decide who each member of the group is.
- As individuals, think about the sort of person you are and how you speak.
- Try to make sure each person speaks for the same amount of time.
- Take turns in speaking and listen carefully to what is said.
- Make sure that what you say follows on from what has just been said, to show you have been listening.

Tip
Each person needs to demonstrate their speaking *and listening* skills. This means following the discussion carefully and responding appropriately.

Tip
To change the direction of the discussion you could say, 'Let's look at this from a new angle.'

Fame

Reflecting on your learning

Speaking and listening

In a group activity, you may discuss subjects as yourself or take on a role and speak as that person. The main objectives are to:

- talk about your experiences, and express your feelings and opinions clearly (as yourself or in a role)
- present facts, ideas and views in a logical order
- use a wide vocabulary
- speak appropriately for the audience and context of the topic
- show you are listening to what others are saying.

Use this guide to help you and to give your classmates feedback.

A. Very good	<ul><li>argues ideas, gives opinions, and is persuasive without dominating the group</li><li>uses a wide vocabulary</li><li>uses an appropriate tone or register</li><li>refers back to previous points</li><li>moves discussion or scene forward with good reasoning</li><li>listens sympathetically and considers the views of others fully</li></ul>
B. Good	<ul><li>makes frequent contributions</li><li>uses a good vocabulary</li><li>uses an appropriate tone or register</li><li>takes part as member of the group but does not move discussion</li><li>may support or oppose new ideas or opinions but rarely starts new ones with sound reasons</li><li>listens carefully and responds briefly but appropriately to others</li></ul>
C. Could do better	<ul><li>brief, infrequent contributions</li><li>sound vocabulary</li><li>plays a limited part in the group</li><li>does not always respond to previous points appropriately</li><li>follows the general drift but rarely introduces new ideas or approaches</li><li>listens inconsistently and may drift off the topic</li></ul>
D. Needs to improve	<ul><li>only makes one or two contributions</li><li>limited vocabulary</li><li>contributions not always appropriate</li><li>does not participate as a member of a group</li><li>may ignore previous points</li><li>does not support or oppose new ideas or approaches</li><li>quiet but shows little evidence of listening</li></ul>

Here are brief extracts of groups discussing the stunt bike advertisement on page 52. Use the success criteria and decide which speakers are participating well, and why the others are not as good.

Group 1 – Jon, Marga, Lorraine and Hassan

Jon: I think we should use the purple bike in the ad.

Marga: I don't see why a girl can't do the stunt.

Hassan: Only purple? What about having two or three different colours – but all doing the same stunt so they don't look as if one colour is better than another.

Jon: Good point. But then we'll need three different riders.

Marga: Girls can do stunts as well, can't they Lorraine?

Lorraine: I don't like purple.

Group 2 – Kieran, Janet, Sofia and Shiv

Shiv: We have two stunt riders doing the same thing in different places, right – like at a competition and in a back garden, that'll show the bike is good enough for comps but ok for kids as well.

Janet: We'd have to set up a whole arena though for a show, it would be very expensive and—

Shiv: So we'll get kids to do it for free. Don't be so negative.

Kieran: That's stupid. We do one stunt in the Rockies with a famous person and that's that.

Group 3 – Julian, Kirsty, Dolores and Sean

Kirsty: I think we should use one bike and do one stunt, but whoever we choose, repeats the competition stunt in a normal street environment.

Dolores: Yes, and have parents watching both and looking pleased and proud.

Sean: What about doing the street scene first, as if the rider is practising, then do it in a competition?

Julian: I saw a mountain bike race with people coming down a rock face in Arizona last week.

Kirsty: Now that's a great idea! What about if we present the stunt in the street then re-create it on a mountain?

4 Leisure and travel

Explore
- a robot hotel
- non-fiction travel writing styles

Create
- a travel blog
- your own humorous image of an animal

Engage
- with juxtaposition and oxymorons
- with ways to create a humorous tone in a piece of writing

Collaborate
- to decide on a dream destination
- to discuss appropriate ideas for a travel blog

In this unit you will:

Reflect
- on the effectiveness of carefully chosen adjectives to create a desired effect
- on the use of hyperbole for effect

So much to see, so much to do.

"The world is a book and those who do not travel read only one page."
St Augustine

"A journey of a thousand miles must begin with a single step."
Lao Tzu

"One's destination is never a place, but a new way of seeing things."
Henry Miller

Thinking time

The number of people who flew on scheduled airline flights in 2014 was slightly under three billion. It is estimated that over 100,000 people fly every day.

1. How many of the iconic structures in the first image can you name?
2. What kind of company would use an image like this one to promote its business?
3. What do you think the third quotation means?
4. Do you think the journey or the destination is the most important part of travelling?

Speaking and listening – Dream destination game

The object of the game is to persuade your fellow group members to agree with your choice of detination.

1. Each member of the group writes down the name of a place they would love to visit one day and five reasons for their choice.
2. Taking it in turns, each member presents their argument by describing their dream destination and explaining why they have chosen it above all others.
3. While this is happening, the other members of the group should be assessing the performance by giving it marks out of five in each of these categories:
    a Does the destination sound appealing?
    b Would you like to go there?
    c How persuasive is the argument presented?
4. The winner is the one who gains the highest mark out of fifteen once all the group members have presented.

Leisure and travel

📖 Robot hotel

Robot hotel: Inside Japan's Henn-na Hotel

by Danielle Demetriou

1   I am sipping tea in a **minimalist** Japanese hotel room while chatting to my personal concierge. She adjusts the lighting, checks the room temperature, sets an alarm call and chirpily informs me that tomorrow's weather will be a little cloudy.

5   This may sound like unremarkable hotel small talk, yet I am transfixed by every word. This is because the "concierge" micro-managing my stay is not a human being. She is a robot.

More precisely, she is Churi-chan, a pint-sized pink and green cartoon-like character with three hearts on her forehead and
10 a permanent smile who sits on my bedside table and tries very hard to be helpful. Churi-chan is one of a number of **surreal** creatures I encounter during my stay at Henn-na Hotel, the world's first robot hotel which opens tomorrow in Japan's southern Nagasaki Prefecture.

15 From check-in staff and porters to cloakroom and concierge, human jobs have been usurped by an **eclectic** cavalcade of robots at Henna-na Hotel, whose name aptly translates as "strange" (although staff prefer the word "evolve"). The bleeping, flashing and perma-smiling robots assume a variety
20 of forms – among them, a long-haired lady humanoid, a head nodding dinosaur and a luggage-toting mechanical limb. Not to forget Churi-chan, one of which sits in each of the 72 rooms – the doors of which, incidentally, open with just a glance, rather than a tiresome key, using facial recognition technology.

25 Behind the scenes are 10 human staff dressed like stagehands in top-to-toe black, who survey the hotel through security cameras and are quick to help with techno blips. Among them is Iwazume Takeru, the quietly spoken hotel manager, who swapped the more conventional Sheraton in Kobe city for his new role.

30 "I was happy to come here, it's an exciting hotel," he enthuses, as we take a stroll through Truman Show-perfect gardens. "I've always been interested in robots, they are the future."

(...)

Word cloud

animated
contemporary
eclectic
eerie
minimalist
surreal

Inside the lobby – an airy modern space with a vast Japanese ikebana flower display in the middle – a colourful cast of robots can be found. First, I see a large white mechanical "cloakroom" arm encased in a glass cube which dramatically retrieves suitcases and places them inside lockers. Next, I spot a bowing humanoid "lady" called Yumeko ("Dream Girl") with long dark hair, **animated** eyebrows and a slightly **eerie** smile who welcomes me in Japanese at the front desk. The English-speaking dinosaur sitting next to her, complete with a bow tie, tiger-like fur and a constantly bobbing head, then informs me with authority: "If you want to check in, push one!"

I proceed to check in, pressing buttons to confirm my identity, before making payment on a touch screen and having my face scanned for room access. I am then instructed to follow my robot "porter" – a mechanical hip-high device carrying my suitcase that rolls at a snail's pace up slopes and along corridors, playing loud disco music and telling me off when I stop walking in a straight line. When we finally reach room 209, I stare at the face scanner – before being firmly rejected. It takes two more goes before I get the hang of it (I have to stand closer, it transpires) and the door finally opens.

Inside, the design in the rooms – as throughout the hotel – is surprisingly tasteful, in a **Muji store** kind of way: **contemporary** minimal Japanese, with expanses of natural woods, simple neutral furnishings and walls of windows.

Against such a backdrop, Churi-chan is impossible to miss: the small cartoon-like robot inspired apparently by a pink tulip sits on the bedside table awaiting instructions from guests. (...)

From *Robot hotel: inside Japan's Henn-na Hotel*,
www.telegraph.co.uk

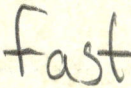

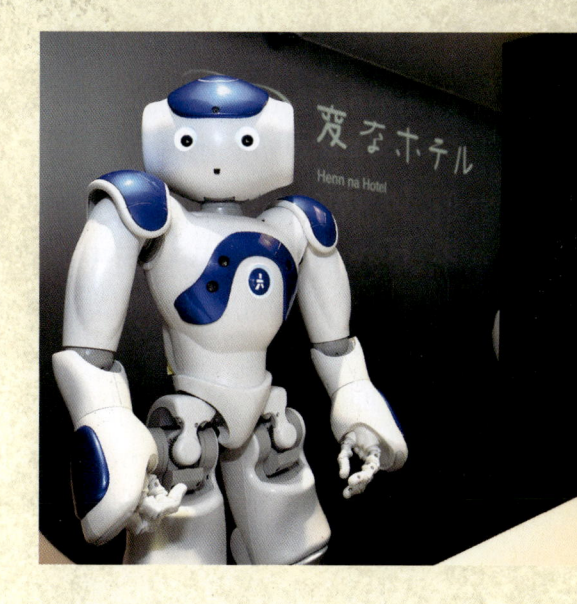

fast

Glossary

personal concierge private receptionist

micro-managing managing the smallest details

Nagasaki Prefecture district of Nagasaki

usurped by an eclectic cavalcade of robots replaced by a varied procession of different robots

perma-smiling permanently happy

Muji store a chain of Japanese department stores

Leisure and travel

Understanding

Henn-na Hotel in Japan is the world's first hotel staffed mainly by robots.

1. In which city is the Henn-na Hotel situated?
2. How many humans work at the hotel?
3. Why doesn't the hotel use 'tiresome' conventional keys to unlock the guest rooms?
4. What evidence supports the view that the writer likes the hotel?
5. Do you agree with the hotel manager that robots 'are the future'?
6. If you were the designer, what aspect of the hotel would you change?

Word builder – setting the tone

The Henn-na Hotel is hoping to attract guests who like science fiction, and specifically robots, so it aims to be different, futuristic and full of technology. The words in the Word cloud are carefully chosen adjectives that together help to describe the mood within the hotel.

1. Given the aim of the hotel, which of the phrases in each string best suggest the tone created by the lead adjective? The first one is completed for you as an example.

   e.g. animated = passive and motionless / active and vigorous / dull and lifeless

   The correct answer is 'active and vigorous' because 'animated' refers to the robots that need to be moving with energy to do their tasks and impress the guests.

   a contemporary = modern and new / old-fashioned and sophisticated / outdated and obsolete
   b eclectic = uniform and predictable / varied and ranging in style / similar and bland
   c eerie = comforting and calming / bright and cheerful / strange and slightly unsettling
   d minimalist = cluttered and homely / essential and what is required / ornate and lavish
   e surreal = ordinary and dull / out of the ordinary and fantastic / real and expected

2. Now it is your turn to create three adjectives to set the mood for these buildings.
   a A deserted office block
   b A busy department store
   c A supermarket

Using adjectives for effect

Carefully chosen adjectives can help the writer to create the atmosphere within a piece of writing.

1. Read the following passage:

   The cavernous room dwarfed the terrified rescuer. Unused as he was to the echoing chamber of the supposedly deserted building, each clattering footstep and skittering rat filled his heart with dread forebodings of his imminent destruction. With his hands shaking with uncontrolled fear, his brow sweating profusely and his teeth chattering in the intense cold, he reluctantly continued on his fruitless search.

2. The adjectives used in this passage raise a lot of questions for the reader.

   e.g. The use of 'cavernous' to describe the size of the room suggests it is very big, so the questions asked are:

   Why is it such a big room?

   What kind of room is it?

   What is its purpose?

   a Make a list of the other adjectives in the passage.
   b Draw four text boxes (or bubbles) and place one of the adjectives in each. Fill the remaining space in each box (bubble) with the questions the reader would want answers to.
   c Choose three of your own adjectives to describe the overall atmosphere created in the passage.

3. Now it is your turn. Write a short paragraph in the style of the one above where your use of adjectives creates questions in the mind of the reader.

Remember

The use of carefully chosen adjectives can bring an image to life and engage the reader by posing questions that require answers. This makes the reader want to read on. The opening paragraph of the 'Robot Hotel' extract is a good example of this useful technique for a writer.

Leisure and travel

📖 Writing to entertain

Our Friend the Moose

1 *Bill Bryson relates the 'sad' case of the endangered moose in North America.*

Goodness knows why anyone would want to shoot an animal as harmless and **retiring** as the moose, but thousands do – so many, in fact, that states now hold lotteries to decide who gets a licence. (...)

5 Hunters will tell you that a moose is a wily and ferocious forest creature. In fact, a moose is a cow drawn by a three-year-old. That's all there is to it. Without doubt, the moose is the most **improbable**, endearingly hopeless creature ever to live in the wilds. It is huge – as big as a horse – but magnificently **ungainly**. A moose runs as if
10 its legs have never been introduced to each other. Even its antlers are hopeless. Other creatures grow antlers with sharp points that look wonderful in profile and command the respect of **adversaries**. Moose grow antlers that look like oven gloves.

Above all what distinguishes the moose is its almost **boundless**
15 lack of intelligence. If you are driving down a highway and a moose steps from the woods ahead of you, he will squint at you for a long minute, then abruptly **hie** off down the road away from you, legs flailing in eight directions at once. Never mind that there are perhaps 10,000 square miles of safe, dense forest on either side
20 of the highway. **Clueless** as to where he is and what exactly is going on, the moose doggedly follows the highway (...) before his peculiar **gait inadvertently** steers him back into the woods, where he immediately stops and takes on a **perplexed** expression that says, 'Hey – woods. Now how (...) did I get here?'

25   From *Notes From A Big Country* by Bill Bryson

Word cloud
- adversaries
- boundless
- clueless
- gait
- hie
- improbable
- inadvertently
- perplexed
- retiring
- ungainly

Glossary
lotteries state-held raffles

drawn by a three-year-old badly drawn

endearingly hopeless lovable but without hope

legs flailing in eight directions with an uncontrolled running action

doggedly follows the highway stubbornly moves along the road

Understanding

Travel writers often present a mixture of facts and personal perspective in their work.

1. Where does the moose live?
2. How do you know hunting moose is a popular pastime?
3. Why do the hunters describe the moose as clever and fierce?
4. How effective is the use of humour in the passage?

Developing your language – creating an image

A successful writer will use a series of ideas to build an image for the reader.

One of the ways Bill Bryson builds his image of the moose as a charming but stupid animal is by using humour to make the creature seem comical.

'a moose is a cow drawn by a three-year-old' – the image makes the shape of the animal seem simple and childish

'A moose runs as if its legs have never been introduced to each other.' – makes the moose seem uncoordinated and clumsy

'he will squint at you for a long minute' – makes the moose sound dim-witted because it takes a long time to understand what is happening

What image does each of these statements suggest?

a   'legs flailing in eight directions at once'
b   'Moose grow antlers that look like oven gloves.'
c   'his peculiar gait inadvertently steers him back into the woods'
d   'Hey – woods. Now how (...) did I get here?'

Word builder

Look at the six adjectives listed in the Word cloud. They are all used to describe the moose in a way that is uncomplimentary and comical.

1. Match the adjective from the Word cloud to the explanation of the effect to build a more detailed unflattering image of the moose as interpreted by the author.

   boundless   it is shy and avoids human contact
   clueless   its lack of intelligence has no limits
   improbable   it is easily confused
   perplexed   it is clumsy and uncoordinated
   retiring   it is difficult to believe an animal like
                  this exists
   ungainly   it has no idea what it is doing

2. a   How much like a real moose is Bryson's comic description?
   b   If the moose could talk what might it say about its life?

Leisure and travel

Using juxtaposition

A *juxtaposition* is when two ideas or concepts are placed next to each other to create a contrast or comparison.

Bill Bryson creates his comical image of the moose using a series of images that are *juxtaposed*.

'Hunters will tell you that a moose is a wily and ferocious forest creature. In fact, a moose is a cow drawn by a three-year-old.'

1. Copy and complete the following table to map the use of juxtaposition.

What the hunters claim	*Meaning*	How the author interprets it	*Meaning*
wily and ferocious		a cow drawn by a three-year-old	*passive and too comical to be dangerous*
it is huge – as big as a horse	*It is powerful and graceful*	but magnificently ungainly	
Other creatures grow antlers with sharp points			*They look soft and fluffy and completely harmless*

2. Now it is time for you to create your own juxtaposition. Choose an animal from the list below:

> Ostrich   Polar bear   Giraffe   Panda   Koala
> Chicken   Sheep   Sloth   Porcupine   Orang-utan

a Make a list of the main features of your chosen animal, both in terms of its physical appearance and personality.

b You are aiming for a comic image so write down an alternative interpretation for each feature in your list.

c Once you are satisfied, write a blog entry about meeting your chosen animal.

d Use your blog entry to play the '30 Seconds' game. The aim of the game is to read out your description without mentioning what animal you've chosen. Your audience must try to guess the name of the animal within 30 seconds of you starting your description.

Using oxymorons

An *oxymoron* is a specific kind of juxtaposition, being a combination of words that appear to contradict each other but, when used together, create an image offering a different meaning.

Bill Bryson uses an oxymoron to create contrast as the moose is described as:

'endearingly hopeless'

He uses 'endearingly' to suggest the moose is an animal that people feel affection for but he contrasts this with the idea of it being 'hopeless', suggesting how pathetic it is.

Normally, you wouldn't be so fond of something that is so useless but Bryson suggests this is one of the reasons why a moose is so likeable.

1. Another oxymoron used is 'magnificently ungainly'.

   Explain the meaning of this phrase and how it works as an oxymoron.

2. Using oxymorons is common among writers. Here are three examples from Shakespeare:

   a 'O brawling love!'   b 'O loving hate!'   c 'Sweet sorrow'

   Explain why each of these is an oxymoron. *Hint: Brawling is another word for fighting.*

3. Here are some more examples of oxymorons. What effect does each one create?

   a bitter-sweet
   b hot ice
   c thunderous silence
   d random order
   e wise fool
   f original copy

4. You can make up some of your own oxymorons. Aim for at least three.

   Just think of an emotion and add an opposite to it, e.g. clearly confused.

Looking closely

Oxymoron is from two Greek words meaning 'sharp' and 'dull', which is itself an example of oxymoron.

Leisure and travel

🎧 Courtesy call

Word cloud
aeon   lunatic
dishevelled mortified
eternity   penitentiary

Glossary
courtesy call a phone call by a company to check a service has been provided appropriately

family solicitor lawyer representing the family

Formula 1 high-speed racing category

taste buds a group of cells on the tongue and in the mouth that identify taste

haul (your company) over the coals severely scold (your company) (an idiomatic expression)

Understanding

Courtesy calls are usually made in order to gauge customer satisfaction, with little expectation that there will be a problem.

1. What is the name of the travel company?
2. Why might Ling have been unsettled by the way the conversation developed?
3. What is your impression of the customer from the way she responds during the call?
4. Does the customer's use of exaggeration support her grievances or detract from them?
5. How might the travel agency representative have handled the call differently and would it have been appropriate to do so?

Word builder – hyperbole

Hyperbole uses exaggeration to emphasise a point. Each word in the cloud is an example of hyperbole.

When she claims that the eight-hour flight took an 'aeon' to complete, the customer doesn't really mean it lasted for an indefinite amount of time but that it seemed to last forever.

1. How are 'aeon' and 'eternity' similar in the effect their usage creates?
2. When she claims the driver looked '*dishevelled* like a tramp' what does she really mean?

3. What image does the use of 'lunatic' suggest when she describes the driver's performance?
4. What do you think the customer means by 'mortified'?

    rigid with fear / embarrassed and humiliated / feeling sick
5. What does describing a hotel as a 'penitentiary' suggest about its treatment of guests?
6. Does the use of hyperbole paint an effective picture of how terrible the holiday was or does it say more about the customer's attitude?

Developing your language – using modal verbs

Modal verbs can be used to indicate if something is possible, probable or certain. They can also be used to make requests and give permission.

The most common modal verbs are:

> can   could   may   might   shall   should   will   would

In 'Courtesy call' the travel agent begins with a polite request:

   Might I take a few moments of your time?

The customer replies with a statement of permission:

   You *may* take some of my valuable time.

Can you recognise the modal verb in each of the sentences below and say what function it is serving?

> **Function:** possible   probable   certain   a request   a suggestion

1. Could it have been any worse, I ask myself?
2. I would like to say it was, but I am afraid I can't.
3. I should warn you...
4. Can we start at the beginning, please?
5. Well, we will definitely investigate what happened.
6. Shall I take you through meal after meal to prove my point?
7. I can assure you that we, as a company, will investigate this matter.

Leisure and travel

✏️ Writing a travel blog

You are going to write a travel blog so it is important to choose a place you *know* well and *like* a lot. Use the writing frame to help you plan.

This extract from a travel blog about Morocco describes a Sunday morning in a village in Ait Bougmez valley:

Key features:
- Non-fiction text
- Personal experiences
- Uses detail
- Colourful and exciting presentation

https://whymorocco.wordpress.com/2015/04/26/a-sunday-morning-in-ait-bougmez/

1 The silence was deafening as I sipped cafe au lait overlooking the peaceful village and the valley below. Men worked the small plots of land by hand, using what seemed to be ancient tools. But an important role as the food produced
5 would nourish the family throughout the summer months and provide a stock for the winter months. The apple and peach trees provided a pop of colour in the already green landscape with the snow-capped Atlas Mountains towering around. Children wandered freely through the village, playing
10 with what little toys they had while the women sat chatting amongst each other. Meanwhile donkeys were led through the village en route to work.

From *Why Morocco?* by Mandy Sinclair

Speaking and listening – the destination game

Find out how much you know about your chosen destination.

Write questions on ten cue cards, e.g. What is the best feature / the most important building / the attitude of the locals / the thing you like doing most / the best time to visit / the most unusual local custom?

Shuffle the cards, then take turns to pick one and ask the question written on it. Your partner has 20 seconds to answer.

Writing frame

Use the guidelines below to plan and draft your travel blog.

Remember that you are writing as if you are in the place being described, so the more convincing you are, the better your blog will be received.

Do your research:
1. Find out about your chosen destination.
2. Make a note of some interesting facts and statistics to use in your blog. Both help to convince an audience you know what you are writing about.
3. Collect some images you can use to highlight the points you make.

   Remember that a picture really does paint a thousand words!

Plan carefully:
1. Decide what details you want to include about your destination – don't try to cram too much in.
2. It is better to highlight a few carefully chosen features than try to cover everything.
3. Before beginning your blog, decide on your paragraph order and where you are going to use your images.

Narrative style:
1. A blog is personal so write in the first person narrative.
2. Keep it fairly informal to create the bond between you and your audience.
3. Adopt a lively, fast-paced style to help persuade the audience they are sharing the experience.

It's all in the detail:
1. You are the audience's eyes. They see everything through your description so make your details count.
2. Use reflection to allow your audience to share your feelings about your experience.
3. Write about the people as well as the place to add another dimension to your blog.

Leisure and travel

Responding to text extracts

How Space Tourism Works

by Kevin Bonsor

1   Make your reservations now. The space tourism industry is officially open for business, and tickets are going for a mere $20 million for a one-week stay in space. Despite reluctance from NASA, Russia made American businessman Dennis Tito
5   the world's first space tourist. Tito flew into space aboard a Russian Soyuz rocket that arrived at the International Space Station on April 30, 2001. The second space tourist, South African businessman Mark Shuttleworth, took off aboard the Russian Soyuz on April 25, 2002, also bound for the ISS. Greg
10 Olsen, an American businessman, became tourist number three to the ISS on October 1, 2005.

On September 18, 2006, Anousheh Ansari, a telecommunications entrepreneur, became the first female space tourist and the fourth space tourist overall. She was also the first person of Iranian
15 descent to make it into space. Charles Simonyi, a software architect, became the fifth space tourist on April 7, 2007.

These trips are the beginning of what could be a lucrative 21st century industry. There are already several space tourism companies planning to build suborbital vehicles and orbital cities
20 within the next two decades. These companies have invested millions, believing that the space tourism industry is on the verge of taking off.

In 1997, NASA published a report concluding that selling trips to space to private citizens could be worth billions of dollars.
25 A Japanese report supports these findings, and projects that space tourism could be a $10 billion per year industry within two decades. The only obstacles to opening up space to tourists are the space agencies, who are concerned with safety and the development of a reliable, reusable launch vehicle.

30 If you've ever dreamed of going to space and doing what only a few hundred people have done, then read on.

From *How Space Tourism Works*, www.howstuffworks.com

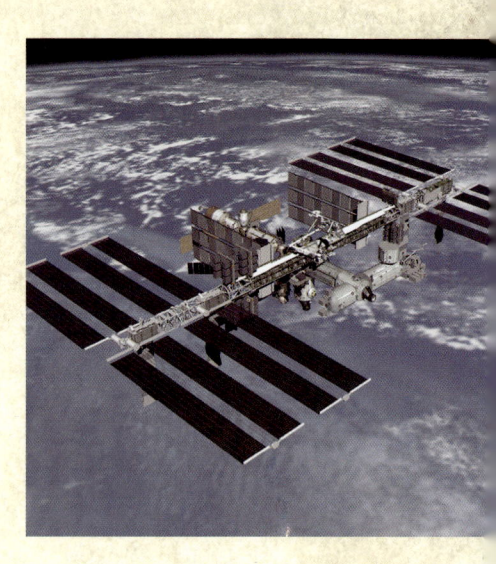

Glossary
NASA North American Space Agency
ISS International Space Station

Forming an overview

Discuss these questions:
1. Who is the intended audience?
2. What is the purpose of the article?
3. What is the overall tone of the article?
4. What is the purpose of using so many facts in the article?

Practice questions

1. Answer these questions on the article.
    a What is the estimated cost of a ticket for a space trip?
    b How long would a trip into space last?
    c What would be the destination for any trip?
2. Suggest a meaning for each of these words in the context of the way it is used in the passage.
    a reservations
    b reluctance
    c entrepreneur
    d suborbital
3. Correct these sentences by adding the necessary punctuation.
    a How do I make a reservation for a trip into space asked the rich businessman
    b Space tourism won't be achievable until the space agencies agree it is safe for it go ahead and a reliable vehicle has been developed replied the travel agent
4. Without using *and* or *but*, turn these three simple sentences into a complex one.

    Space tourism is exciting.

    It is very expensive.

    It will be more popular in the next two decades.
5. List the space tourists who have travelled so far and what their nationalities are.
6. Write a response to the article in which you argue that space tourism will not become a popular leisure activity. Use the article for your ideas but try to use your own words as far as possible.

    Write 80–100 words.

Leisure and travel

Sample responses to space tourism article

Here are three sample responses to question 6.

Kimi

Space tourism wont become a popular lesure activity because it costs a lot of money to take a space trip. 20 million dollors. Only a few hundred poeple have been into space. They are all rich poeple. It is dangerus and NASA don't like it happning very much. There are a few companys putting money into space trips but none have made a space ship that can do it so you cant go yet. NASA don't like it becose it is dangerus and the tourism can be killed and that would be bad and not good.

Fozia

Companies have spent millions on space tourism but it may all be wasted because the technology to build a reliable vehicle is not available. This is a massive problem as without this spaceship the tourists will not be able to voyge to the space station. Furthermore it is not thought to be safe enough by NASA so it is unlikely to go ahead. There is also the question of cost. There are very few people in the world who can afford to spend twenty million dollars on a hobby so will there ever be a variable market for space tourism.

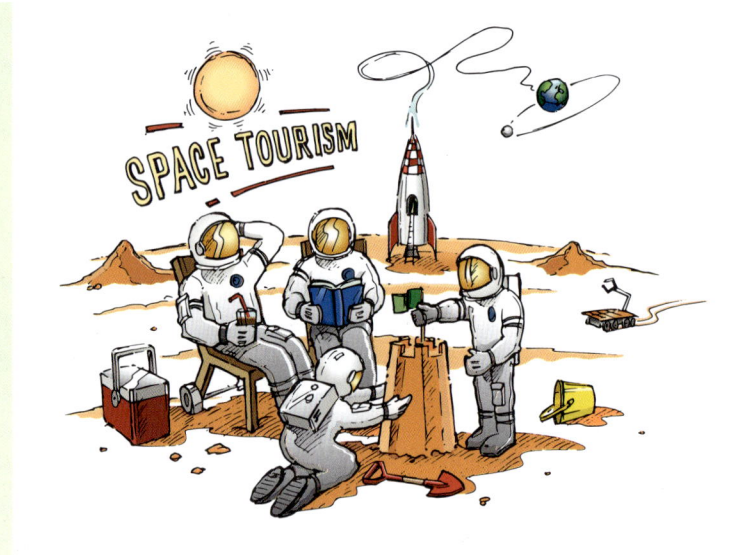

Melissa

However appealing space tourism for you and me may appear it is not a reality that will occur for many decades to come. The absence of a safe and dependent vehicle capable of making indefinite voyages to and from the International Space Station suggests the technology is lagging way behind the imagination of the companies investing huge sums of money in the project. Even if such a mode of transportation was available, space tourism remains a pipedream until the space agencies deem it sufficiently safe and logistically manageable. Those who have already travelled as space tourists will remain the rich and fortunate ones for the foreseeable future.

Teacher commentaries on sample responses

Here are the three teacher commentaries for the responses but the order has been rearranged.

> *The word count is just outside the guidelines but this should not detract too much from the positives experienced in this reponse. The tone is appropriate and the focus on the task is sustained throughout. The sentence structure is mature and allows the ideas to flow appropriately. Punctuation is used correctly although there is a limited range being used. Spelling is very accurate across a good range of vocabulary including more difficult low-frequency words.* — Melissa

> *The word count is within the guidelines. The response shows a good grasp of the question and sustains an appropriate focus throughout. All the response is relevant and it is controlled with some skill. There is a range of sentence structures evident that are confidently expressed. Punctuation is generally accurate throughout – there is a question mark missing at the end – though limited in range. There is one spelling mistake but 'voyage' should be considered a more difficult word. The writer confuses 'variable' and 'viable'.* — Fozia

> *The word count is within the guidelines. A genuine attempt has been made to answer the question and there is a general focus that is maintained throughout the response though there is also some unnecessary repetition. There is little sense of audience but a suitable tone is used. The sentence structure is basic, with overuse of common connectives in the last two sentences. The punctuation is limited but not entirely accurate, especially the use of apostrophes. Spelling is more problematic, with several words misspelt that should not have been. There is little attempt to use more difficult words so the range of vocabulary employed is also limited.* — Kimi

1. Match the commentary to the response.
2. Share with a partner a list of the key points you have understood by reading the commentaries.
3. Rewrite your own response, taking into account your new understanding.

73

5 Exhilarating exploration!

In this unit you will:

Explore
- why people travel to remote places
- different features of text types

Collaborate
- to create a holiday island
- to take part in a survival game

Create
- a holiday brochure
- a newspaper article

Engage
- with a story of a boy who swims with a dolphin
- with the experience of travelling along the Amazon

Reflect
- on what makes for good group work
- on different ways of varying sentences for effect

"These days there seems to be nowhere left to explore, at least on the land area of the Earth."
Carl Sagan

"Every new city or country or continent that I visit is a beautiful exploration from which I can learn."
Andrea Michaels

"Exploration is experiencing what you have not experienced before."
Richard Aldington

74

Thinking time

Use the images and quotations on the opposite page to help you think about the following:

1. What words do you associate with the idea of exploration?
2. Do you know the difference between 'travel', 'exploration' and 'adventure'? Can you come up with a definition for each word?
3. Do you think it is possible to be an explorer in the traditional sense today? If so, where would you like to explore and why?

Speaking and listening

Exploration does not have to involve exploring a place – it could be about exploring ideas or experiences.

1. Working with a partner, give a 30-second presentation to the class on three ways you can explore without travelling anywhere!
2. The class should give feedback to each pair and then vote on which idea is the most interesting.

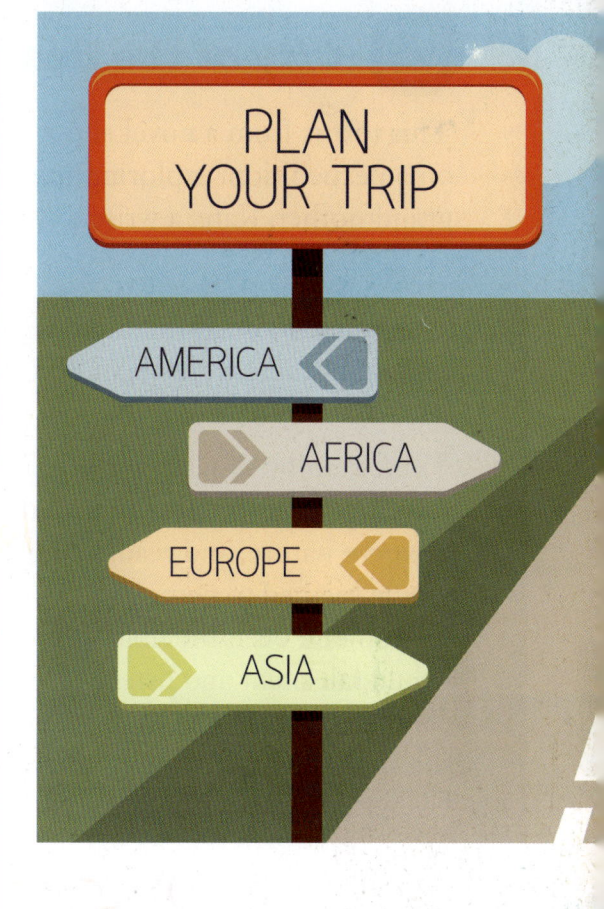

What are the features of different text types?

You are going to be exploring a number of different text types. Below are some of the features of different text types.

includes description of setting   uses connectives to show sequence of steps

has an address at the top   uses the present tense   has persuasive language

uses connectives to link arguments   had direct address to the reader

contains commands   has a headline   often written in the past tense

includes technical language   uses passive constructions   includes many adjectives

written in the third person   uses rhetorical questions   written in the first person

1. With a partner, make a list of as many different text types as you can.
2. On your own, choose one text type and make a list of its features. Use some of the suggestions above and add your own ideas.
3. Now share your ideas with your partner. Are there features that are common to different text types?

Exhilarating exploration!

📖 City of the Beasts

This text is from a novel about a boy called Alex, who is on an expedition, exploring the Amazon on a boat with his grandmother, Kate, a writer.

1   The jungle loomed threateningly on both banks of the river. The captain's orders were clear: do not wander off for any reason; once among the trees, you lose your sense of direction. (…)

    Time went by slowly, hours dragging into **eternity**; even so,
5   Alex was never bored. He would sit at the prow of the boat and **observe** nature, and read, and play his grandfather's flute. The jungle seemed to come alive and respond to the sound of the instrument; even the noisy crew and the passengers on the boat would fall silent and listen. Those were the only times that Kate
10 paid any attention to Alex. The writer was a woman of few words; she spent her day reading or writing in her notebooks (…) Everything about this trip was so different from the world Alex had grown up in that he felt like a visitor from another galaxy. Now he had to do without comforts he had always taken for
15 granted, like a bed, a bathroom, running water, and electricity. (…)

Word cloud
douse   queasy
eternity   radiant
observe   torrential

Glossary
caboclos a Brazilian of mixed ancestry

His most serious problem was food. He had always been a picky eater, and now they were serving him things he couldn't even name. (…) One day the crew shot a couple of monkeys, and that night when the boat was tied up along the riverbank they were roasted. (…) Alex felt **queasy** just seeing them. The next morning they caught a *pirarucú*, an enormous fish that everyone but Alex, who didn't even taste it, thought was delicious. (…)

Several times a day a brief but **torrential** rain fell and the humidity was horrendous. Alex had to get used to the fact that his clothing never really got dry and that after the sun went down, they were attacked by clouds of mosquitoes. The foreigners' defence was to **douse** themselves in insect repellent (…). The *caboclos*, on the other hand, seemed immune to the bites.

On the third day, a **radiant** morning, they had to stop because there was a problem with the motor. While the captain tried to repair it, everyone else stretched out in the shade of the roof to rest. It was too hot to move, but Alex decided it was a perfect place to cool off. He jumped into the water, which looked as shallow as a bowl of soup, but he sank like a stone beneath the surface.

'Only an idiot tests the bottom with his feet,' Alex's grandmother commented when he came to the surface streaming water from his ears.

Alex swam away from the boat (…). He felt so comfortable that when something quickly brushed by his hand he took an instant to react. Not having any idea what kind of danger lay in store (…) he began to swim as fast as he could back toward the boat, but he stopped short when he heard his grandmother yelling not to move. (…) He floated as quietly as possible and then saw a huge fish at his side. He thought it was a shark, and his heart stopped, but the fish made a quick turn and came back, curious, coming so close that Alex could see its smile. This time his heart leaped, and he had to force himself not to shout with joy. He was swimming with a dolphin!

From *City of the Beasts* by Isabel Allende

Exhilarating exploration!

Understanding

1. Find two words in the first paragraph which make the jungle sound dangerous.

2. The writer shows that there were aspects of the trip that Alex enjoyed and aspects which he didn't enjoy so much. Summarize in two lists the enjoyable and the less enjoyable aspects of the trip.

3. What impression do you get of Alex's grandmother, Kate? Support your ideas with quotations from the text.

4. How does the writer structure the final paragraph to build up to the last sentence?

5. Identify the features of this extract which show that it is from a narrative text.

Word builder

1. Look at the words in the Word cloud on page 76. How many of them do you know? Write a dictionary definition for one that you know the meaning of. Follow this pattern:

> **Selfie (OED)**
> - noun – plural 'selfies'
> - informal
> - a photograph that one takes of oneself, typically with a smartphone, and posted to a social media website.
> - origin early 21st century: from self + -ie.

2. Have another look at the words you don't know the meaning of. Re-read the sentence where each one appears in the text. Try to work out from the context what each word means. Then check your answers in the dictionary. Add any words that are new to you to your personal vocabulary list.

Key concept

Figurative language

Writers use figurative language to help create vivid pictures in the reader's imagination as they read. Figurative language includes:

- **Similes** – where something is compared to something else, using 'like' or 'as'
- **Metaphors** – where something is compared to something else, without using 'like' or 'as'
- **Personification** – where something is described as though it is a person/human
- **Alliteration** – where words which start with the same sound are deliberately placed together

Developing your language – identifying figurative language

1. Which of the following, from the text, is an example of: a simile, personification, or alliteration?

    a 'The jungle seemed to come alive and respond to the sound of the instrument' *Personification*

    b 'He jumped into the water, which looked as shallow as a bowl of soup' *Similie*

    c 'the humidity was horrendous' *Alliteration*

2. Look at the section of text below. What do you notice about the length and structure of sentences the writer uses?

1 'Alex swam away from the boat (...). He felt so comfortable that when something quickly brushed by his hand he took an instant to react. Not having any idea what kind of danger lay in store (...) he began to swim as fast as he could back
5 toward the boat, but he stopped short when he heard his grandmother yelling not to move.'

3. Look at the last sentence. The writer could have written:

    'He began to swim as fast as he could back toward the boat, not having any idea what kind of danger lay in store but he stopped short when he heard his grandmother yelling not to move.'

    How is the effect of this version different? Why do you think the writer chose to write the sentence in the way she did?

79

Exhilarating exploration!

🎧 Explorers and expeditions

Why do people become explorers and go on expeditions? Is it exciting or terrifying or both? Listen to the discussion between Adil and Nenet about exploration.

Understanding

1. Adil and Nenet have different views about explorers and exploring the world. Explain how their views are different.
2. Explain two ideas about people exploring remote places that they agree about.
3. What do the following quotations mean?
    a. 'go off and push the boundaries of what is possible'
    b. 'not making your mark on a place but allowing that place to make a mark on you'.
4. Who did you agree with more – Nenet or Adil – and why?
5. Can you find examples of what Nenet and Adil say which show that they are listening to what each other says?
6. Has your opinion of exploring and exploration changed as a result of listening to this discussion?

Word cloud
addictive   hostile
countless   new
dangerous   remote
famous   wonderful

Developing your language – identifying sentence types

When we talk, we use a range of 'sentence types'. Sentence types include statements, questions, commands and exclamations.

1. Can you match each of the following to a sentence type?
    a. 'I'd love to become an explorer, like Benedict Allen.'
    b. 'Why on Earth would anyone want to do this?'
    c. 'How awesome is that!'
    d. 'You are right about that.'
2. Why is it easy to spot questions and exclamations?
3. In speech, people don't always speak in complete sentences. Can you find three examples of incomplete sentences from the discussion between Adil and Nenet?
4. What other features of spoken English do you notice when you listen to Adil and Nenet? How is spoken English different from written English?

🔍 Looking closely

A rhetorical question, like 'Hey, did you know?', is a question directed at the reader or listener which does not expect an answer. It is designed to get the audience's attention, introduce an idea or make them think.

Word builder

Look at the words in the Word cloud. 'Addictive' is an adjective which often has a negative meaning, as it may mean doing too much of something and not being able to stop even when the consequences could be harmful.

1. Name the word classes for the other words in the Word cloud. Look up definitions in a dictionary if words are unfamiliar.
2. Divide the words into those that create a positive impact and those that create a negative impact. Are there any words which could be either positive or negative?
3. Can you spot any other words from the same word classes in Nenet and Adil's discussion?

Speaking and listening – group discussion

Imagine you have got lost in the Amazon jungle. Decide as a group which six of the following items would be most helpful in enabling you to survive. You have five minutes to come to a unanimous decision!

> **Tip**
>
> We use language differently in speech and writing. Sentence boundaries aren't as important in speech as they are in writing, as we can always explain what we mean.

Insect repellent   A compass   A map   Matches   A knife

A tarpaulin   A sleeping bag for each person

One pack of energy bars   Water purifying tablets

A cigarette lighter   A book on edible plants in the jungle

A mobile phone   A hammock for each person

A first aid kit   A spare change of clothes for each person

Now evaluate how effectively you collaborated to get this task done.

81

Exhilarating exploration!

Varying your sentence structure for effect

It is important to use a range of sentences to make your writing interesting. This means using different sentence types, lengths and structures.

We are going to look at some ways of varying your sentences. Sometimes this will affect the meaning; sometimes, it will alter the emphasis or impact.

A. Changing the order of clauses in a coordinated sentence, for example:
- He was surprised and reached out to touch the dolphin.
- He reached out to touch the dolphin and was surprised.

B. Changing the position of the subordinate clause in a complex sentence, for example:
- Although they sometimes take risks, explorers help us to understand more about the world we live in.
- Explorers, although they sometimes take risks, help us to understand more about the world we live in.
- Explorers help us to learn more about the world we live in, although they sometimes take risks.

C. Putting the subject near the end of the sentence, for example:
- In the depth of the water, several yards away from them lurked a massive alligator.

D. Starting with a non-finite/-ing verb, for example:
- Sweating, she pushed her way through the jungle.
- Hiding behind a tree, he watched the elephant.

E. Starting with an adverb or adverbial, for example:
- Later, sitting round the campfire, they discuss the day's adventures.
- For many weeks, they tried to rebuild their boat.

Now answer the following questions.

1. **a** What is the difference in meaning and effect between the two sentences under heading A above?

   b Try linking the clauses below in different ways, using different coordinating conjunctions: **and**, **but** and **or**. Look at the meaning and impact of each one. (You may find some don't really make sense!)

         Alex ate the fish   Alex felt sick

2. **a** What is the difference in emphasis between the three sentences under heading B opposite?

   b Try rewriting the sentence below with the subordinate clause in different places. What is the effect in each case?

   It is difficult to find a part of the world that hasn't been explored, unless you are very determined.

3. **a** What is the effect of putting the subject at the end of the sentence? Try rewriting the sentence under heading C with the subject at the beginning. Does this sentence have a different effect?

   b Try writing two sentences with the subject at the end.

4. Try writing two sentences which start with a non-finite verb.

5. Try writing two sentences which start with an adverb or adverbial.

6. Now combine the clauses below into sentences. Aim to use some of the different structures you have been practising and try out different ways of combining the clauses.

the boat drifted as	the trees whispered in the breeze
it drifted along the river	the trees looked as though they were moving
the river was deep	Alex leaned over the side
the river was dark	he saw an alligator
the river was mysterious	the alligator was sliding
on either side was the jungle	the alligator was sliding through the mud
the trees hung over the river	it looked as though it was smiling

> **Tip**
>
> There are lots of different ways to express your ideas in sentences. You can choose how you do this to create the effect you want!

Exhilarating exploration!

📖 Comparing text types

First man to hike Amazon River ends two-year, 4,000-mile trek

1. British explorer Ed Stafford finished his two-year, 4,000-mile trek along the Amazon River on Monday, completing a feat never before accomplished (…). The hike, which he started at Camana, Peru, on April 2, 2008, ended Monday at Maruda Beach, Brazil.

5. Four months after he started, he was joined by Peruvian forestry worker Gadiel "Cho" Sanchez Rivera. Sanchez intended only to guide Stafford for five days through a dangerous area near Satipo, Peru, but stayed to the end of the expedition. (…)

"I'm more tired and more **elated** than I've ever been in my
10. life," Stafford said (…). "We've lived through some very serious situations and there have been times when we genuinely feared for our lives, but we never ever thought of giving up. The fact that everyone told us it was impossible spurred us on.

"At first it was **terrifying** but it's changed in our eyes during the
15. expedition and a place that was once **mysterious** and dangerous to us is now a place where we feel safe. (…) It's not a scary place for us now; it's **beautiful**; we've fallen in love with it. (…)"

Despite collapsing from exhaustion on a roadside Sunday morning, Stafford had been confident he would finish in time
20. Monday to catch a scheduled flight home (…).

It's the kind of fortitude that Stafford has summoned time and again since setting out from the Amazon's River source to raise international attention about rain-forest destruction and to help raise funds to combat it. (…)

Adapted from article on www.edition.cnn.com

Word cloud
beautiful   mysterious
elated   terrifying

Glossary
feat an achievement which requires great courage, skill or strength

spurred urged on by

fortitude courage when facing difficulties

Understanding

1. In what way is the first paragraph typical of a newspaper article?

2. Explain two ways you can tell Stafford's achievement was remarkable.

3. Apart from the first paragraph, identify the features of this text that are typical of a newspaper article.

84

Come and experience a Peru Amazon Rainforest family adventure!

1 Peru's Amazon rainforest is the perfect adventure playground for families looking for an educational and exciting holiday.

Our family programmes for kids – choose from 3,
5 4, 5 days or longer – focus on being educational and entertaining at the same time, and suitable for both children and their parents.

Kids can explore trails around the comfortable eco-lodge, following the story of a six-year-old
10 girl (…) called Ania. Adults are welcome to join in, but can also choose to do their own activities.

The lodge, comfortable, accessible and well-designed, is built on a private **reserve** on the Tambopata National Reserve. It is becoming
15 **integrated** into the **communities** of Brazil nut extractors, to extend the benefits of ecotourism.

It's the perfect destination for families wishing to explore and enjoy Peru's Amazon rainforest!

Adapted from www.responsibletravel.com

Word cloud
communities   reserve   integrated

Glossary
Brazil nut extractors people who extract oil from Brazil nuts

ecotourism tourism which supports the conservation of places and their wildlife

Understanding

1. Why do you think the writer uses the phrase 'adventure playground' in the first paragraph?
2. Explain three ways this text tries to appeal to parents.
3. What do you notice about the first and last paragraphs?

Remember
Adjectives are words that modify or describe nouns. Synonyms are words with the same meaning, for example, *happy* and *cheerful*.

Word builder

Look at the adjectives in the Word cloud on page 84. Write down as many synonyms for each of the words as you can.

Exhilarating exploration!

Writing a travel brochure

Travel brochures are designed to persuade people to visit somewhere, but also to give them important information about the place.

You are going to write a travel brochure for a holiday on a remote, exotic island.

1. In small groups, create your imaginary island and think about what goes into a travel brochure. You need to decide:

   - where your island is
   - how big it is
   - what geographical features and wildlife it has
   - what the climate and weather are like
   - the kinds of holidays this island offers
   - who they are aimed at
   - the accommodation and activities available.

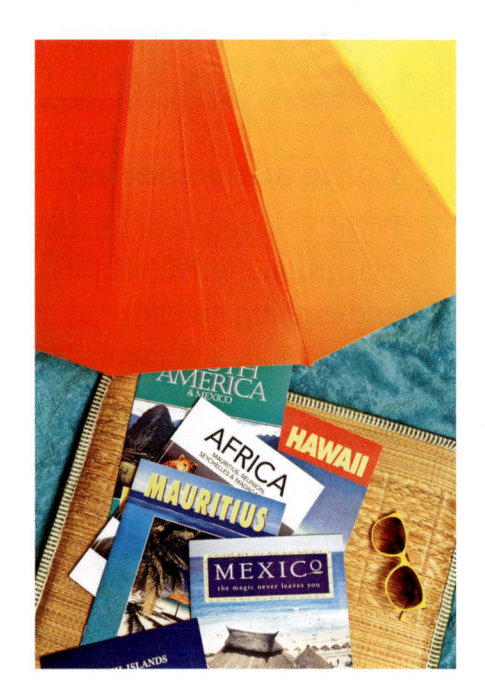

2. Copy and complete the grid below to help you think about the features used in travel brochures.

Feature	Hint/clue	Ideas
Heading	What is the purpose of the heading in a travel brochure?	
Organization	How is the content in a travel brochure organized?	
Style	What kind of style are travel brochures written in?	
Range of sentence types and structures	What sentence types and structures do travel brochures include?	
Language features	What kind of language features might you include in a travel brochure?	
Which word classes are very important in travel brochures?	How might you use noun phrases, pronouns and adjectives in particular?	

3. Now read the guidelines on the next page and write your own travel brochure, persuading people to have a holiday on your island.

> **Remember**
> - choose a suitable heading
> - organize your ideas appropriately
> - use a range of linguistic and grammatical features and vocabulary.

Planning

Write a plan for your travel brochure. Make sure that your plan shows:

- how you are going to begin and end your brochure
- what is going in each section
- some ideas for language features and vocabulary.

Writing

As you write, go back to your plan to make sure that you are keeping to it, or if you aren't, it's because you have had a better idea. Re-read what you have written at the end of each paragraph or section, aloud or in your head, to check that it makes sense. If you are not happy with a word or a sentence, cross it out and change it.

Proofreading

This is the last stage in the process, where you check very carefully to make sure every detail is correct.

Use the checklist below to help you to proofread your travel brochure.

- Is what you have written organized clearly and in a coherent way?
- Are there clear sections or paragraphs?
- Is each sentence clear, with appropriate punctuation?
- Have you used capital letters where necessary?
- Is your spelling correct, including homophones?

Go back to your plan and make sure you have checked your specific targets, for example, apostrophes or the spelling of 'there', 'their' and 'they're'.

Editing

When you have written a first draft, read it through aloud to see what it sounds like. You may find you want to:

- reorganize sections or sentences
- delete sections or sentences
- add sentences or sections
- change your opening or ending
- delete, change or add words to sentences.

Remember – deleting unnecessary words and sentences is just as important as adding extra ones.

Exhilarating exploration!

Non-narrative writing – article for a newspaper

You have read two texts about exploring the Amazon. You will now write an article for a national newspaper about a group of young people who got lost while on a trek in the Amazon but managed to find their way back to safety.

You could include some of the following in your article:

- a summary of key information about what happened
- a more detailed account of what happened to the group of young people
- comments from the young people, their parents and other relevant people
- any other relevant information and ideas.

For this type of question, you need to start by thinking about:

- the purpose and audience of the article
- the details of what happened – how many young people, how long were they lost for, what adventures they had
- the features of a newspaper article you want to include.

You also need to keep in mind the writing skills you will be assessed on:

- content, purpose and audience
- text structure
- sentence structure and punctuation
- spelling.

When writing an exercise such as this on paper, allocate some planning space to jot down your ideas and plan how you are going to organize your article. Remember, it is important to have effective first and last paragraphs as those are what the reader tends to remember.

You can plan your writing in a number of different ways. Here are some possible approaches.

- Locals amazed at resourcefulness of young people
- Young people to give talks about importance of survival skills
- Three friends lost in jungle after a plane crash. 10 days. Broken ankle. Ate berries. Chased by jaguar. Bitten by mosquitoes. Fell into animal trap.
- Parents very proud
- Don't forget headline and paragraphs!

Headline

Summarize main points – eight teenagers on school trip, wandered away from boat into jungle and couldn't find river, made a camp and fire and so on, found way back to river, boat gone but followed river to village to get help.

Main

Explain why they were on the trip, how they got lost, details of what happened (good and bad) with comments from teacher (left on boat), parents and one or more of the teenagers. Include comment from expert in survival?

Ending

How they got home, what they did next, what happened back at school, how future trips will make sure this doesn't happen again – safety arrangements.

Need to include a good ending that links back to the first paragraph

Now plan and write a response to this task.

Remember

Be sure to follow the stages of the writing process:
- plan
- draft
- edit
- proofread.

In your writing remember to:
- use a variety of sentences
- punctuate comments as direct speech
- check spelling.

Exhilarating exploration!

Reflecting on your learning

Non-narrative writing

Here are two responses to this task. In a group, decide which is better, and why.

Then individually, or in pairs, mark each of the responses, using success criteria. When you have done this, share your ideas for each response.

For the answer that is weaker, discuss and agree some constructive and detailed advice for the writer. Remember to refer back to the **task** and to the **success criteria** to make sure that what you are saying is specific and focused.

Tomasz
Amazing Amazon Adventure!

On Friday 7th November a group of students from City College got lost in Amazon jungle. They had to use their survival skills to make their way back to camp and meet up with the rest of the group. They did this and it was all fine in the end.

It started one evening; when two students, Lia and Sen were drawn into the jungle by the strange sound of an animal. What could it be, they were thinking. So they decided to go and have a look. After a while, they realised they couldn't see any of the rest of the students. Then two other students who heard them shouting came after them and then they got lost too. The girls were crying and they didn't know what to do.

Suddenly, one of them said 'I have a compass. We can use this to find out way back to the river. They made a kind of tent to sleep in overnight and the next day they used the compass to find the river. 'It was scary but awesome,' says Lia, but her mother says that 'she wants to go travelling again!'

Nadia

Lost in the Amazon

A group of kids were travelling in the Amazon when they get lost. This happened because they were looking at some insects, they forgot to follow the leader. This was because they saw some amazing butterflies as they were walking along. Their parents were very worried, they didn't know what to do. 'I am hoping my son is safe said one mother.' She wanted to go and look for him in the Amazon.

In the end the young people were safe. They kept by the river. They ate flowers and looked after each other. When they are arriving back to the city yesterday. It all ended happily.

It was a frightening experience. I was really scared and didn't know what to do. We decided to keep together and we made a camp, we caught some fish for food. We lit a fire so people could see us and we were lost for three days. One day, we had a good idea and we followed a river to get home.

After you've analysed Nadia and Tomasz's responses, using the marking criteria, rework your own answer to improve it.

Keep checking that you are following the task brief and showcasing your writing skills to meet the criteria you will be marked against.

6 Rights and freedom

Explore
- the role of the United Nations
- your writing style

Create
- a piece of writing that is argumentative
- a successful oral presentation

Engage
- with the advantages of using topic sentences
- with the early life of Nelson Mandela

Collaborate
- to recognise the differences between concrete and abstract nouns
- to recognise and use discourse markers

In this unit you will:

Reflect
- on the work of Médecins Sans Frontières
- on the validity of the 'Mozart effect'

'United Nations – it's your world'

The United Nations is committed to protecting the basic human rights of every human person in every nation, large and small.

Intellectual intelligence is the first step to freeing ourselves from our physical bonds. To really be free we must all make the most of our intelligence.

"For to be free is not merely to cast off one's chains, but to live in a way that respects and enhances the freedom of others."
Nelson Mandela

Thinking time

The United Nations is dedicated to preserving peace in the world.

1. Why do you think there is a map of the world on the UN flag?
2. Suggest why the seating is set out in a circle in the General Assembly room where members of the UN meet.
3. Why is it important to respect the rights and freedom of others?
4. How can using your intelligence lead to personal freedom?

Speaking and listening

UN flag rationale

The United Nations flag was designed in 1946 and adopted by the UN on 7th December of that same year. The flag consists of a 'flattened' globe, representing all the countries in the world, bisected in the centre by the Prime Meridian and divided into five concentric circles. It is surrounded by a wreath made of branches from an olive tree to further represent peace.

1. You are going to design your own Freedom Flag. Using the UN flag rationale as your guide, in your group:

    a Discuss what the idea of freedom means to you and what your flag should represent.

    b Discuss ideas for the flag and reach a general agreement as to what the flag should contain.

    c Consider:
    - What colours to use
    - What symbols to include
    - What writing, if any, should be included

2. Design your flag.
3. Prepare a short group presentation to share your ideas as to what your flag represents and why it should be displayed.

Glossary

'flattened' globe a two-dimensional image of the planet

Prime Meridian an imaginary vertical line of longitude set at 0°, from which all other lines of longitude are measured

Rights and freedom

A balanced argument?

Unlocking the 'Mozart effect'

1   Almost everyone has heard of Mozart, but did you know that he was an accomplished pianist and violinist by the age of five? Not only that, but he began composing symphonies soon after, and had completed over 600 works by the time of his death at only 35. There is no doubting that Mozart was a musical genius, but in recent times a theory has come to light that suggests his music might inspire genius in others.

So what is the 'Mozart effect' and how does it work? It is a phrase that was coined by renowned otalaryngolist and inventor Alfred A. Tomatis in the early 1990s, and later developed as a theory by US music critic and teacher Don Campbell. Writing in the journal *Nature*, Campbell **theorised** that brain power could be increased as a result of listening to Mozart, and demonstrated this with higher IQ scores in a test group. Although the effect was only temporary, it was enough to **arouse** widespread attention.

After all, who wouldn't want to be smarter given half the chance? The study certainly captured the interest of the mass media, and was soon reported widely and viewed by many who read about it as entirely **plausible**. It proved particularly popular with parents of young children, perhaps hopeful that they might have a prodigy in the making if their child listened to enough **sonatas** before bedtime.

In the US, it was reported that the Governor of Georgia wished to allocate public funds so that children born in the state would be sent a classical music CD. The magic of Mozart was truly casting its spell.

In the years that followed, right up to today, the 'Mozart effect' has remained a popular theory, even though research has not always come out in its favour. For every study that claims improved **spatial** reasoning, there are just as many that point out flaws and lack of foundation in the original logic. Where effects have been observed they are only temporary and, some might say, of minimal use. However,

Word cloud

arouse   sonatas
cortical   spatial
plausible   theorised

Glossary

come to light to be discovered, and widely shared

otalaryngolist a physician specialising in ear, nose and throat diseases and disorders

mass media newspapers, television, the internet, radio and magazines

prodigy a highly talented young person

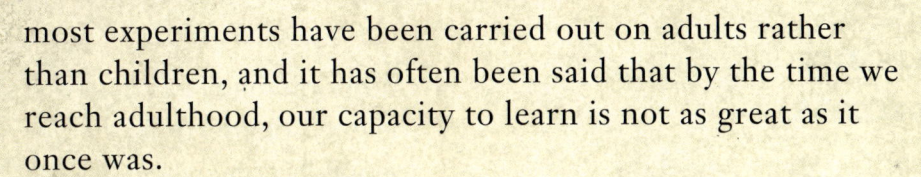

most experiments have been carried out on adults rather than children, and it has often been said that by the time we reach adulthood, our capacity to learn is not as great as it once was.

Where does that leave us today? As recently as 2015, the *Daily Mail* reported that researchers from the Sapienza University of Rome had linked listening to Mozart with improved memory function in young adults and the elderly. Interestingly, there were no such effects in those who listened to Beethoven, leading the researchers to speculate that particular patterns in Mozart's music 'activated' **cortical** circuits of the brain. Furthermore, in a separate study by the University of Electronic Science and Technology of China, rodents with epilepsy were exposed to the music of Mozart, and their mental processing vastly improved as a result, which could suggest a positive application for humans with a similar condition.

Perhaps that means there is something in the 'Mozart effect' after all? It would be good to think that even now, more than 300 years after his death, Wolfgang Amadeus Mozart is helping others through his music. And even if it can't make everyone who listens to it instantly smarter, at least we can enjoy it for what it is – beautiful, timeless music.

Understanding

In the article, the author considers whether the 'Mozart effect' has an effect on our level of intelligence.

1. In your own words, what is the 'Mozart effect'?
2. Who was Mozart?
3. Why were the particular patterns in Mozart's music thought to have an effect on the brain?
4. In what ways did people react to the original study, and why?
5. Do you think the author believes in the 'Mozart effect'?
6. Can you think of some conditions that are likely to bring out our intelligence?

Rights and freedom

Word builder – using low-frequency words

Low-frequency words are those that are considered more difficult to understand and are used less by writers.

All six words in the Word cloud would be considered of low frequency.

Sometimes more difficult words can be identified because they look and sound like root words which are more commonly used. Also, the words that surround it can offer clues to its meaning.

Remember

Although many words have synonyms that generally convey a similar idea, be careful when using synonyms as the original word may imply something slightly different. Choosing the correct word will add precision to your writing.

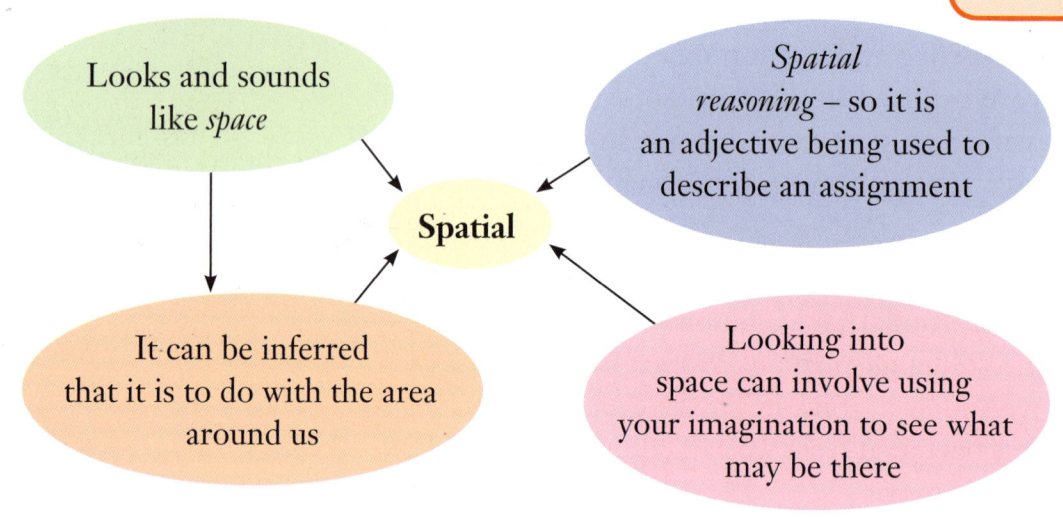

- Looks and sounds like *space*
- *Spatial reasoning* – so it is an adjective being used to describe an assignment
- **Spatial**
- It can be inferred that it is to do with the area around us
- Looking into space can involve using your imagination to see what may be there

Indeed, **spatial reasoning** tests require the student to mentally rotate and re-order objects without being able to physically touch them.

1. Use the same process used to explain *spatial* and apply it to the word *theorised*.
2. Can it be used for any of the other four words in the Word cloud? Give reasons for your answers.
3. Use a dictionary to look up the precise meaning of *cortical* and *sonata*.
   a. What more common terms could be used in their place?
   b. How would the use of the more common terms detract from their meaning in the passage?

Tip

One of the ways you can write for greater effectiveness is to expand your vocabulary and use a wider range. Used correctly, these low-frequency words help to create a more mature writing style.

Developing your writing – using topic sentences

A topic sentence:
- is the first sentence in a paragraph
- introduces the main idea in the paragraph.

A topic sentence is useful because:
- it focuses the writing within the paragraph
- it acts as a summary of the points in the paragraph.

This is the first sentence in the article.

Almost everyone has heard of Mozart, but did you know that he was an accomplished pianist and violinist by the age of five?

It is an effective opening because:

Almost everyone has heard of – suggests you have prior knowledge because this subject is important enough to be well known.

but did you know – involves the reader by leading them into the topic and presenting an interesting fact.

an accomplished pianist and violinist by the age of five? – introduces the main theme of the article with an example of a child genius.

The rest of the paragraph consists of two related sentences.

Sentence	Writer suggests	Reader
2	Mozart achieved much in his short lifetime	reflects on what they have achieved or might achieve in that time
3	Mozart's music inspires genius in others	is interested in whether it could have that effect on them

1. Write down a list of topic sentences for the rest of the article.
2. Look at the last paragraph beginning 'Perhaps that means…'. Copy and complete the table below to show how the paragraph is developed.

Sentence	Writer suggests	Reader
1	The 'Mozart effect' might have some truth to it	Reflects on what they have read in the article
2	It is a good thing because it helps those who need it	

Key points

Topic sentences can be used to introduce paragraphs in all kinds of writing, including argumentative, persuasive and narrative.

Writing a series of topic sentences can be an effective way of planning a piece of writing.

Rights and freedom

📖 Doctors without borders

Médecins Sans Frontières

An introduction

1 Médecins Sans Frontières (MSF) is an international, independent, medical humanitarian organisation that delivers emergency aid to people affected by armed
5 conflict, epidemics, natural disasters and exclusion from healthcare. MSF offers assistance to people based on need, irrespective of race, religion, gender or political **affiliation**.

Our actions are guided by medical **ethics** and the principles of
10 **neutrality** and **impartiality**.

A worldwide movement

MSF was founded in Paris, France in 1971. Its **principles** are described in the organisation's founding charter. It is a non-profit, self-governed organisation.

15 Today, MSF is a worldwide movement of 24 associations, bound together as MSF International, based in Switzerland.

Thousands of health professionals, logistical and administrative staff – most of whom are hired locally – work on programmes in some 70 countries worldwide.

20 **Humanitarian action**

MSF's work is based on humanitarian principles. We are committed to bringing quality medical care to people caught in **crisis**, regardless of race, religion or political affiliation.

MSF operates independently. We conduct our own evaluations
25 on the ground to determine people's needs. More than 90 per cent of our overall funding comes from millions of private sources, not governments.

MSF is neutral. We do not take sides in armed conflicts, we provide care on the basis of need, and we push for independent
30 access to victims of conflict as required under international humanitarian law.

www.msf.org/about-msf

Word cloud

affiliation   impartiality
crisis   neutrality
ethics   principles

Glossary

Médecins Sans Frontières (MSF) Doctors Without Borders

humanitarian organisation a group committed to improving the lives of others

medical ethics moral code based on the doctors' oath

self-governed organisation independent of governments

international humanitarian law as defined by the United Nations

Understanding

The passage opposite is taken from the home page of the Médecins Sans Frontières website.

1. What kind of organisation is Médecins Sans Frontières?
2. Where is MSF International based?
3. How is it a neutral and impartial organisation?
4. Why do you think 'humanitarian' is used four times in the passage?
5. What is the importance of MSF remaining independent of any particular government?
6. In pairs, suggest an organisation you would create in order to help others.

Word builder – abstract nouns

Nouns can be *concrete* or *abstract*. Unlike *concrete* nouns, *abstract* nouns are the names of things that cannot be perceived by one of the five senses.

1. All six words in the Word cloud can be classed as abstract nouns as they are all concepts. Take each noun in turn and do the senses test. Can you see, touch, hear, taste or smell any?

2. With a partner, take turns to describe three objects in the room without using their concrete nouns. Can your partner guess what they are?

3. Here are some more abstract nouns:

    anger   bravery   comfort
    freedom   hope   imagination
    opportunity   success   thought
    trust   truth   wisdom

    Take turns to choose three of these abstract nouns and explain their meaning to a partner without naming them. Can your partner guess what they are?

4. Which was most difficult to explain and guess? Why do you think this is so?

Rights and freedom

Key concept

Transitions

Transitions are words and phrases used to connect ideas in writing. They are often linked with connectives because they have similar roles in written work. **Example:**

I knew that to be an active member of Médecins Sans Frontières would take hard work, skill and courage but I volunteered immediately I had the opportunity to do so.

Here, the transition used is immediately because it indicates the time when the doctor made the decision to join MSF.

Transitions are used to:

Order/sequence ideas
e.g. first of all
secondly
finally

Show cause and effect
e.g. consequently
as a result
hence

Add information
e.g. in addition
furthermore
moreover

Indicate place
e.g. beyond
in the background
adjacent to

Indicate time
e.g. presently
subsequently
immediately

Compare
e.g. equally
similarly
in the same way

Contrast
e.g. and yet
on the contrary
alternatively

Give examples/show emphasis/illustrate
e.g. namely
in particular
illustrated by

Conclude
e.g. to conclude
to summarise
on the whole

Identifying transitions

Identify the transition in these sentences.

1. Médecins Sans Frontières is guided by strong medical ethics in addition to a desire to help all people.
2. MSF raised millions of dollars from appeals last year and subsequently helped millions of people.
3. The positive effect that MSF has achieved can be illustrated by the awards it has achieved worldwide.

Why transitions are important

The difference between transitions and connectives is that transitions define more closely the connection between ideas in your writing.

Look at these two simple statements about charities:

They need money. They help people.

Now add two transitions:

First they need money **then** they help people.

Using **first** and **then** enables the reader to clearly understand the order of events.

> Here are some more transitions:
>
> additionally   regardless   nevertheless   undoubtedly   in order to
> in conclusion   elsewhere   likewise   temporarily   clearly
> specifically   above all   for instance

1. Copy and complete the statements by using appropriate transitions from the box. All of the transitions have been used once.

   a. The doctors treated the wounded _____ of the shells falling around them. _____ the nurses were also in danger.

   b. _____ save lives _____ the charity has to be well organised.

   c. Helping refugees, _____ in Sudan, _____ relieves their suffering; _____ a more permanent solution is needed.

   d. Doctors give their services free of charge but _____ the medicines they use are very expensive so funds must be raised _____ and _____ by using the internet. _____ the cost of transporting aid to where it is needed is expensive so while the doctors are working _____ support workers are trying to raise funds.

   e. _____ I would say that MSF does a wonderful job.

2. Make a list of all the transitions mentioned on this page.

   a. Look through the written work you have done over the last seven days and add a tick by the relevant transition for every time you have used it.

   b. When you have completed your review, consider whether you are using enough transitions in your writing or whether you should be using more.

> **Tip**
>
> Use transitions to connect your ideas and make your writing more precise.

101

Rights and freedom

🎧 Nelson Mandela – the early years

Sara is about to deliver a presentation to her teacher on the early life of Nelson Mandela, a political leader in South Africa who became the first black president of the country. She is using a cue card but no other notes. This is the first time she has presented this topic formally but she has been practising at home.

Word cloud
- admittedly
- essentially
- frankly
- predictably
- understandably
- undoubtedly

Understanding

1. What was Nelson Mandela's given first name at birth?
2. Where was Nelson Mandela born?
3. Which two incidents in his early adulthood showed Nelson Mandela was not afraid to challenge authority if he thought his cause was just?
4. Although the presentation is based on a serious subject, Sara is not afraid to use humour in her responses in the discussion. How does she do this?
5. Which other famous personality would you consider to be an inspiring subject? Give reasons for your choice.

Glossary

cue card brief notes used as an aid to memory

kraal a homestead surrounded by a wall

rondavel a round hut made of soil baked into bricks

apartheid a system of segregation based on ethnic origin

African National Congress a political party in South Africa

Key concept

Discourse markers

Although discourse markers can appear in different forms of writing, they are more often found in examples of both formal and informal speech. Generally, if the discourse marker is removed from the phrase, the sentence will still be grammatically correct.

Discourse markers are used:

- To begin a topic in a conversation – *'Right, I want to talk about Mandela.'*
- To refocus a conversation – *'on the other hand'*
- As fillers or to delay speaking – *'you know', 'well'*
- To offer minimal feedback during a conversation dominated by the speaker – *'exactly', 'absolutely', 'yes, I agree'*
- To focus attention on what is to come in the sentence – *'As far as I am concerned...'*

Using discourse markers

Identify the discourse markers in the following interaction between a teacher and his student.

'Now then, we've all heard of Nelson Mandela but on the other hand how many of you knew his given first name was Rolihlahla? How about you Rohit, did you know?' Amid much shaking of heads from the rest of the class, Rohit timidly replied. 'No sir, well, I always thought it was Nelson, you know, because that's what they call him on the news channel, please sir. As far as I am concerned, that's his name, sir.'

Word builder

The words in the Word cloud are also discourse markers. This time they signal the attitude or point of view being expressed.

Copy the lists and match the six words to the correct attitude or point of view intended.

Definite, without question	Admittedly
Expected, given the circumstances	Essentially
Logically, based on what is known	Frankly
Confessing agreement	Predictably
Being honest and plain speaking	Understandably
Expressed in a basic way	Undoubtedly

Tip

Discourse markers can be very effective when they are used appropriately or very distracting when they are not, so it is important to recognise them.

Rights and freedom

✎ Writing to present an effective argument

You are going to write a six-paragraph argumentative essay for the school's magazine, exploring this question:

Should pupils be able to listen to music whilst studying in class?

Planning your response

Use these boxes to guide you. They do not necessarily have to be completed in this order.

Consider the question
- ✓ Decide where you stand on this subject.
- ✓ Think of four points in support of your opinion.

Consider the target audience
- ✓ Adopt a suitable tone – provocative/dismissive/pleading?

Form your topic sentences
- ✓ Turn these into four topic sentences.
- ✓ This will be the main body of your essay.

Think about the counter-argument
- ✓ What is it?
- ✓ How is it weaker?
- ✓ What proof can you use?

Opening paragraph
- ✓ Practise some introductory sentences.
- ✓ Aim for something that *grabs* the reader.

Concluding paragraph
- ✓ Have a clear idea about where you stand on the question.
- ✓ Aim for a memorable last sentence.

💬 The 'Prove it!' game

Play the game using the following rules.

1. Player 1 states a point.
2. Player 2 challenges by shouting 'Prove it!'
3. Player 1 then has to offer evidence to support his/her point.
4. If Player 2 is not satisfied, he/she continues to shout 'Prove it!' until sufficient evidence is provided.

Writing frame

Paragraph 1 – Introduction:
- Begin with a strong comment.
- Give an overview of the argument, introducing the four points you are going to use to support your opinion.
- Make sure the reader is aware of how you stand on the question.

Paragraphs 2 – 4:
- In turn, expand on the four ideas introduced in your opening paragraph.
- Prove your opinion.
- Consider one point per paragraph.
- Introduce each with a topic sentence stating the key point.
- The rest of each paragraph should prove the key point.

Paragraph 5 – Counter-argument:
- Introduce the counter-argument.
- Explain why it isn't as strong as your argument.

Conclusion:
- Sum up your argument.
- End with a strong comment that the reader will remember.
- Link back to opening points.
- Ensure your viewpoint is consistent with that expressed in the introductory paragraph.

Remember to use

- Transitions
- Topic sentences
- Low-frequency words

Remember

When making a point:
- Clearly state the point.
- Support it with evidence to provide proof.
- Offer an explanation that backs up the evidence.

Rights and freedom

Designing and delivering a sustained talk

In some ways *designing* a sustained talk is the same as writing a longer essay:

- The goal is to successfully communicate a series of connected ideas to the audience.
- The text is written in sentences that are grammatically correct enough to express meaning.
- The text is divided into paragraphs that each deal with a separate point and, ideally, are introduced using topic sentences.
- Success is based on the quality of the content and how well it is presented to the audience.

It is the *delivery* that differs:

- Written texts are delivered through the indirect medium of words on a page punctuated effectively so the reader can create the voice of the writer internally.
- Oral presentations create a *direct link* between the presenter and the audience.

1. Create two columns headed 'Engaging' and 'Unengaging'. With the audience in mind, work out where to list each of these characteristics of a talk.

   *lively   dull   read from a script   rehearsed   a range of intonation   fluent
   thoughtful   one-paced   a range of linguistic devices   monotonous   discourse markers
   articulate   considered   rushed   important points emphasised*

2. Imagine you have been tasked with designing a five-minute talk on one of the following:
   - My rights as a student
   - My responsibilities as a student

   Write an opening paragraph for your talk. This will involve planning and organising your ideas.

3. Present your opening paragraph and listen carefully to the resulting observations regarding how engaging it is.

4. Now write the rest of the talk.

5. Prepare your talk for delivery. Practise using a range of intonation.

> **Remember**
>
> An opening paragraph should outline the points that are to be made in the rest of the talk so it acts as a kind of 'super' topic sentence.

💬 A focused discussion

You have written your talk and prepared to deliver it successfully.

After you have delivered your talk to a passive listener, you will be asked to discuss the content.

This discussion could last for five minutes so detailed responses are required.

Preparing for the discussion

Although you will not know what questions will be asked and what direction the discussion will take, you can have some control over it.

- Think of 5 or 6 questions that might be asked about the content of your talk. Think about your answers to each one. Try to extend these answers to last for 20–30 seconds each.
- Often the questions asked will be a direct result of what you say in the discussion, so only introduce points if you are willing to discuss them.
- Don't be passive and wait for the next question. Ask your own questions and be prepared to fill pauses with your own comments.

Open and closed questions

The response will always depend on the kind of question asked.

Closed questions are easier to answer but difficult to expand beyond the basic response. 'Do you believe students should have rights?' is a closed question as it requires a 'yes' or 'no' response.

- Can you think of 5 more closed questions concerning your talk?
- What will your answers be?

Open questions are more effective as they allow you to offer opinions and expand upon your initial answer. 'Why are student rights so important to you?' is an open question as it doesn't have a 'yes' or 'no' answer.

- What is your response to this open question?

Look back at the questions you created when you first started thinking what people might ask about your talk. How many were open questions?

Rights and freedom

Meliz and Rebekah each decided to prepare a four-minute talk on the subject of 'school rules'.

The three criteria were:
- awareness of their target audience – i.e. the teacher
- including suitable but challenging content
- offering a balanced persuasive argument.

Below are the openings from their talks:

Meliz

> I am going to talk about school rules. I don't think school rules are fair. Most of them don't make sense and are just annoying. I don't know anyone who thinks they are fair. I don't know anyone who likes wearing the school uniform. It's just stupid. You have to wear a blazer in class all the time and it is uncomfortable. In the summer it's too hot and in the winter it's too cold. I'd rather wear a hoody or a pullover when it's cold. When it's hot the blazer is too warm and suffocates you. The teachers won't let you take them off in class and I think that's stupid too. What does it matter if you don't wear a blazer? The world's not going to end!

Annotations:
- Immediately on task
- Clear perspective given but expressed in functional language rather than a more mature style
- Very simple comment with no supporting evidence provided
- Becoming a series of personal complaints rather than a reflective overview of all the key issues.
- Already repetitive and vocabulary lacks sophistication
- Syntax is basic and argument doesn't flow so audience interest lost.
- This is just another rant in the making so the content continues to be thin and uninspiring.
- Clearly animated and engaged which is good. Is the humour intentional or a by-product of the rant?

Rebekah

Immediately on task, reflective and offering a valid perspective in a considered tone

I understand the need for school rules and I know we can't be without them but I have to say some of them are really frustrating. In my talk I'm going to cover some of the rules I think are good and work well and others that aren't so effective. I'm going to offer some alternatives to the ones I feel are flawed and suggest ways in which students and the school authorities can work more closely together to improve the rules for everyone concerned.

I'd like to start with the school uniform as this seems to be the biggest concern for some students. I actually think the uniform is about right.

Clearly sets out premise of talk and offers a balanced view

The vocabulary is used soundly and the syntax is sufficiently mature to allow the talk to flow. As a result audience interest is being maintained

This is a measured, planned and organised reply and considers the wider perspective in a reflective way

The level of vocabulary is appropriate without being particularly sophisticated. It is more than merely functional

Maintains personal engagement with the topic without resorting to ranting

1. Discuss the relative merits of each talk based on the criteria.
   a Which talk do you think is better?
   b Give reasons for your choice.
2. Now check your findings by considering these qualities. Assess each response on whether:
   a The talk has been planned and structured for effectiveness.
   b The talk is appropriate for the target audience.
   c The talk offers a balanced and considered argument.
   d The level of vocabulary used is challenging.
   e The tone of the talk is measured and analytical.
   f The talk is persuasive.
   g The talk is engaging and I want to hear the rest of it.

7 Poetic predators

In this unit you will:

Explore
- the depths of the Maldive sea
- the forests of the tiger

Create
- a story about an encounter with a snake
- a factual entry for a webpage

Engage
- with thinking about a shark's teeth and your teeth
- with poems as art forms

Collaborate
- to write a group poem about predators
- in a discussion about poetry

Reflect
- on the similarities and differences between two poems
- on which of a group of poems you think is the best

Oh, those eyes!

"Poetry is a mirror that makes beautiful that which is distorted."
Shelley

"The poets have been mysteriously silent on the subject of cheese."
G K Chesterton

"A poet's work is to name the unnameable, to point out frauds, to take sides, start arguments, shape the world, and stop it going to sleep."
Salman Rushdie

110

Thinking time

1. Think of as many ways as possible in which a poem differs from a story. Is there anything a poem can do better?
2. Can poets write about subjects like cheese, or should poetry be about things like flowers, rivers and mountains? Can you think of an unusual subject for a poem?
3. What does Salman Rushdie mean by all of the items he lists in a poet's work?

Speaking and listening

Predator – The group poetry game

A predator hunts or preys on other creatures. Here are some: hyena, wild boar, crocodile, leopard, king cobra, piranha fish, grizzly bear, grey wolf, shark, komodo dragon.

Begin by finding out some facts about these animals. Make notes that you could use.

The game is to make up a poem.

- Choose a predator. Decide how many lines to have in your poem – you may change your mind, particularly if the poem works well and you want to go on.
- The leader starts with a single line of five words, like 'I am a king cobra'.
- The next person adds a line of five words, perhaps ending with a word that rhymes, or would be easy for someone else to rhyme with.
- Carry on round the group, each person adding a line of five words. Someone will have to write the poem down.
- When you want to end the poem, make a line that everyone can shout together.
- Perform your poem.

You may want to use several lines to describe your animal: its eyes, its teeth, the sounds it makes, how it moves and, in general, how frightening it is. That could help you with your last line.

Remember the golden rule – choose your words to make the best effect. You can add alliteration, onomatopoeia, similes and metaphors.

Poetic predators

📖 The snake experience

Discuss: Before you read these two poems, think what you would write about if someone told you to write a poem about a snake. What do you think about immediately someone says 'Snake!' to you?

Decide how you want to read these poems aloud – remember not to pause until you come to a punctuation mark, or you might lose the meaning.

Medallion

1 By the gate with star and moon
   Worked into the peeled orange wood
   The bronze snake lay in the sun

   Inert as a shoelace; dead
5 But **pliable** still, his jaw
   Unhinged and his grin crooked,

   Tongue a rose-coloured arrow.
   Over my hand I hung him.
   His little vermillion eye

10 Ignited with a glassed flame
   As I turned him in the light;
   When I split a rock one time

   The garnet bits burned like that.
   Dust dulled his back to ochre
15 The way sun ruins a trout.

   Yet his belly kept its fire
   Going under the **chainmail**,
   The old jewels **smouldering** there

   In each **opaque** belly-scale:
20 Sunset looked at through milk glass.
   And I saw white maggots coil

   Thin as pins in the dark bruise
   Where his innards bulged as if
   He were digesting a mouse.

25 Knifelike, he was chaste enough,
   Pure death's-metal. The yardman's
   Flung brick perfected his laugh.

                         Sylvia Plath

Glossary

medallion a large medal, usually worn round the neck as an ornament

tongue a rose-coloured arrow his tongue was the shape and colour of a rose-coloured arrow

as if he were digesting a mouse 'were' is an unusual tense and is used only when the idea is impossible

yardman works in a storage yard, loading and unloading equipment and doing minor repairs

To the snake

Green Snake, when I hung you round my neck
and stroked your cold, **pulsing** throat
as you hissed to me, **glinting**
arrowy gold scales, and I felt
the weight of you on my shoulders,
and the whispering silver of your dryness
sounded close at my ears –

Green Snake – I swore to my companions that certainly
you were harmless! But truly
I had no certainty, and no hope, only desiring
to hold you, for that joy,
which left
a long wake of pleasure, as the leaves moved
and you faded into the pattern
of grass and shadows, and I returned
smiling and haunted, to a dark morning.

Denise Levertov

Word cloud

arrowy	opaque
chainmail	pliable
glinting	pulsing
inert	smouldering

Understanding

1. What is the most obvious similarity between the two poems and how are they different?
2. Explain what is happening in each poem and in what sense they are reflective (that is, how they represent the writers' thoughts). What is important about the ending of each poem? Especially in 'To the snake' why is the writer 'haunted' and why is the morning 'dark'?
3. Discuss how each writer addresses the snake, the first calling it 'he' and the second 'you'. Why is it important to the poems that the snakes are not addressed as 'it'?
4. Titles are important when you write a poem (or a story). Discuss what you think of the titles of these two poems.
5. Imagine you are the yardman in 'Medallion'. Write what you would say about the events that make up the poem. You are talking to some friends.

Looking closely

Poems often contain plenty of imagery but one of the two poems has very little and the other has a lot. You'll notice that imagery is used because the writer wants us to see exactly what she saw when she picked the dead snake up. Imagery should be used for a purpose.

Poetic predators

Word builder

A word in your word cloud is 'smouldering'. Sylvia Plath compares the colours and the shapes of the snake skin to jewels and speaks of 'The old jewels smouldering there'. She could have said 'shining', which just describes a bright light. 'Smouldering' gives a deeper picture of a glowing light, burning away, which may suddenly break out into a more exciting and glittering colour – like a flame.

Explain these words.

1. Why is '*arrowy* gold scales' better than 'pointed' in 'To the snake'?
2. Why is 'cold, *pulsing* throat' better than 'moving' in 'To the snake?'
3. What does 'chainmail' add to the picture of the snake's skin in 'Medallion'? Why not just say 'scales'?
4. What effect does '*inert* as a shoelace' have when the writer could have said 'still'?
5. Why would 'bendy' be a bad choice of word instead of 'pliable'?

Developing your language – writing about an encounter with a snake

To describe something really well you need to think of your own word cloud before you begin. Here are some more snake words that you might be able to find.

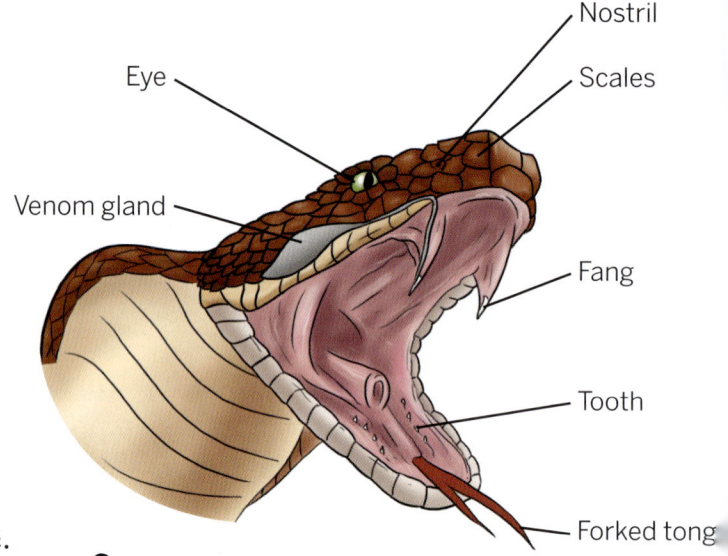

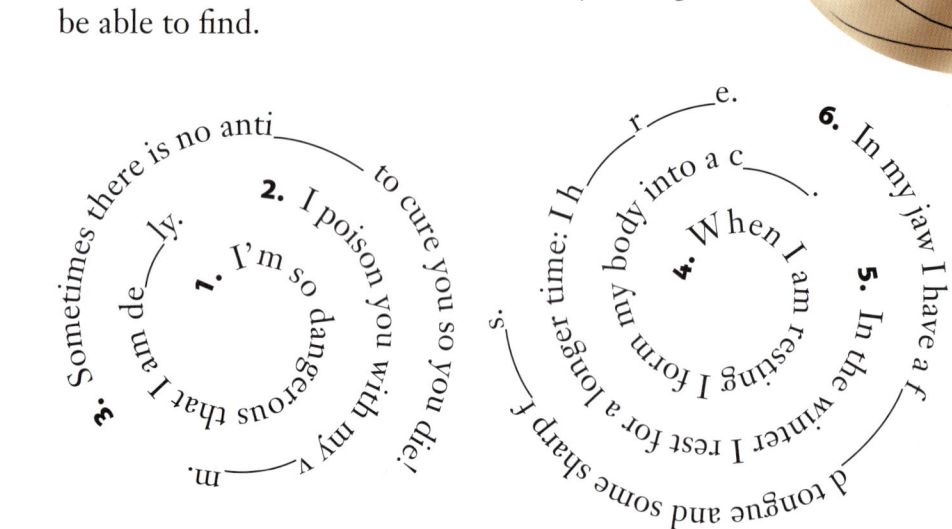

1. I'm so dangerous that I am de___ly.
2. I poison you to cure you so you die!
3. Sometimes there is no anti___ to my v___m.
4. When I form my body into a c___e.
5. In the winter I rest for a longer time: I h___te.
6. In my jaw I have a f___d tongue and some sharp ___s.

Imagine you suddenly discover a snake. Write two paragraphs. In the first, describe what you see and hear and in the second, what happens. Remember to include your feelings at the time and afterwards.

Developing your language – writing from notes

Here are some notes made from researching snakes. The notes are in the writer's own words and are not copied from the source. They are in no particular order.

1. Long, no legs, eat animals (no veg), are reptiles
2. Use smell to find prey – forked tongue collects particles
3. In all continents except Antarctica (not Ireland or New Zealand)
4. 20 families – length varies from 10cm to nearly 7 metres
5. Most non-poisonous – rare human deaths, but some amputation
6. Find prey by sensing vibrations in the ground
7. Usually avoid humans – venom used for catching prey and digesting it, not self-defence
8. Skin scaly – NOT slimy! (people think it is)
9. Some live in sea (Indian Ocean and Pacific)
10. Skulls have joints so can swallow prey bigger than head
11. Prey – lizard, frog, bird, egg, fish, snail

Imagine someone has set up a website about predators and has asked you to write a short entry on the topic of snakes. It has to be factual, not a story or a description. You have found all sorts of interesting facts which are listed above.

Use the facts to write your entry.

To help you:

- **Beginning and end:** Which items are best to start and to finish?
- **Get the best order:** For example, there are three notes about snakes' prey; these will have to go together.
- **Develop the wording of your notes:** For example, in item 8 you could write 'People often mistakenly think …'.
- **Write your own words:** Develop your own style, as in item 3: 'Snakes are found in nearly every corner of the world…'.

Remember

Never copy whole sentences and phrases from the Internet, encyclopedias, or textbooks. Always try to develop your own style of writing.

Poetic predators

'The Tyger' by William Blake – a poem for discussion

Here are two students, Abellia and Rashid, talking about the first verse of a very famous poem. Their teacher has asked them to prepare a reading of the verse, but they have decided to begin by working out what the writer is saying to them.

The whole poem is printed below. You will need it later for your own discussion and reading.

Understanding

1. Why did Abellia think that Rashid's first attempt at reading the verse was not good enough?
2. How do you know that William Blake meant his tiger to sound scary?
3. Blake said the tiger was 'burning bright', which makes him sound as if he were on fire. How did Rashid explain what Blake imagined?
4. What did Abellia and Rashid say and do about the two examples of alliteration in the first verse?
5. Do you think this poem was written for children or adults? Explain what you think.

The Tyger

1   Tyger Tyger, burning bright,
       In the forests of the night;
       What immortal hand or eye,
       Could frame thy fearful symmetry?

5   In what distant deeps or skies,
       Burnt the fire of thine eyes?
       On what wings dare he aspire?
       What the hand, dare seize the fire?

       And what shoulder, what art,
10   Could twist the sinews of thy heart?
       And when thy heart began to beat,
       What dread hand? what dread feet?

What the hammer? what the chain,
In what furnace was thy brain?
What the anvil? what dread grasp,   15
Dare its deadly terrors clasp?

When the stars threw down their spears
And water'd heaven with their tears:
Did he smile his work to see?
Did he who made the Lamb make thee?   20

Tyger Tyger, burning bright,
In the forests of the night:
What immortal hand or eye,
Dare frame thy fearful symmetry?

William Blake

💬 Speaking and listening – thinking about delivery and meaning

Discuss the fourth and fifth verses of 'The Tyger' and prepare to read them aloud.

It isn't easy to decide how to discuss a poem. Think carefully about the things that Abellia and Rashid talked about. You could start with the meaning of the verse as a whole and then go through it line by line.

You could talk about how you feel when you read it, what the words mean and why you think the writer chose them. You might discuss the length of the lines, the rhythm, the rhymes and tricks such as alliteration, onomatopoeia, or any images.

When you listen to a poem, what are you listening for?

When you read it aloud, what sort of voice should you use?

For verse four, Abellia and Rashid might ask each other these questions. They may help you, but try to ask some of your own as well.

Rashid: Why do you think there are so many question marks?

Abellia: These words, 'hammer', 'chain', 'anvil' and 'furnace' – what do they have to do with a living tiger?

Rashid: We said that the first verse was scary. Is this verse still scary?

Abellia: Have you ever heard the story of Frankenstein, the guy who created a monster he could not control? Doesn't the fifth verse sort of make you think of that? If I could create animals and people, I wouldn't make a creature like this tiger.

Rashid: You mean you'd just make creatures like lambs and bunny rabbits! Yes, but why does Blake suddenly bring the lamb into it anyway?

When you have finished, read the fourth, fifth and last verse. The last verse is the same as the first – or is it?

You might also be able to read the whole of the poem to finish this session.

Poetic predators

Punctuation – punctuating your complex sentences

Proofread the paragraph and find places to put ten full stops and eight commas.

To help you, these are the conjunctions that are used in the paragraph: *if, when, while, because, since, which, as.*

> **Remember**
>
> A main clause is a sentence within a complex sentence. Subordinate clauses are joined to it by conjunctions such as 'because'. They do not make sense by themselves.

Life is short. Smile while you still have teeth!

1 If people don't look after their teeth properly they run the risk of having fillings or losing them altogether count up your teeth most of you when you have all your adult teeth have a total of 32 the front chisel-shaped teeth are called
5 incisors they are used for cutting your food while the ones with sharp points are your canines they tear the food because you need to crush your food you have eight pre-molars with two pointed cusps finally since a lot of foods have to be ground into little bits you have a set of molars they include
10 four wisdom teeth which come later wisdom teeth can be a real nuisance to a lot of people as they become impacted.

Teeth dialogue:

Bigtooth: So I can't join sentences with 'this', 'I', 'he', 'she', it' or 'they'?

Minitooth: No, none of those because they are pronouns and not conjunctions. You can't use 'then' either. Look, I'll show you: 'My dentist is a cheerful lady. She makes jokes all the time I'm sitting in her chair.'

Bigtooth: I see. So it's a full stop after 'lady' and not a comma.

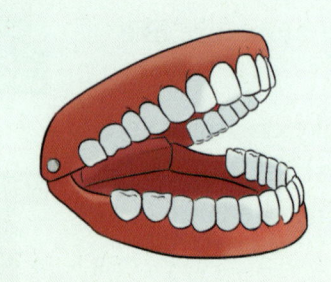

Here's some writing called 'My dentist is not a predator'.

1. Explain why the full stops are where they are and why any commas have been used.

A long time ago, before you were born, going to the dentist was quite a frightening experience because dentists didn't have today's technological marvels. You sat in an uncomfortable chair and waited while the dentist scoured your mouth for signs of decay, which was stressful. Sometimes he would pull your mouth into strange shapes and then shake his head sadly. He'd get a pair of pliers and pause dramatically before entering your mouth, grab the offending tooth, and pull as hard as possible.

Minitooth says: I put a full stop after 'technological marvels' on line 3 because the next sentence begins with 'you', which isn't a conjuction. I put commas round 'before any of you were born' because it interrupts the flow of the first sentence.

2. What's wrong here?

Nowadays people don't worry about dentists, they are kind. They don't use old-fashioned tools on your teeth, they have super-fast drills that operate quickly and painlessly. You rest on a sort of bed, it is really comfortable comfortable enough for relaxation. The best thing to do is not to drink sugary drinks, then your teeth won't decay and the enamel won't wear off.

Minitooth says: Put a full stop after 'dentists' because 'they' is a pronoun, not a conjunction. Then join them together by saying 'Nowadays, people don't worry about dentists as they are kind'. 'As' is a conjunction.

Find three other wrongly punctuated pairs of sentences. Say why the commas are wrong and use conjunctions to join each pair together.

Decide whether you need extra commas. Sometimes you should split up a complicated sentence, but often a comma disturbs the flow.

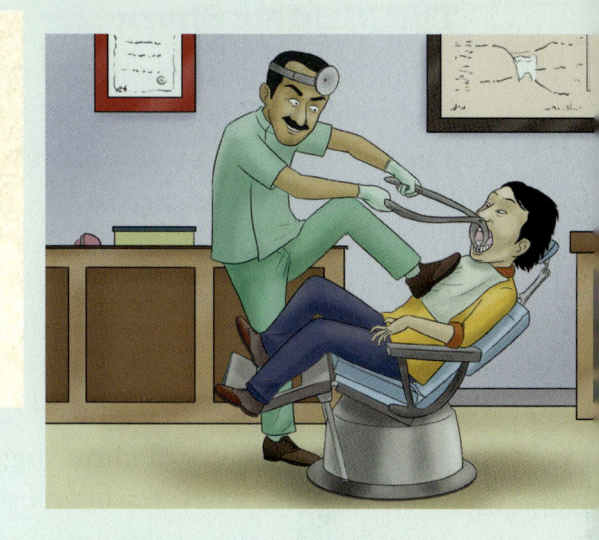

Poetic predators

A predator of the sea

The Maldive Shark

1   About the Shark, phlegmatical one,
Pale sot of the Maldive sea,
The sleek little pilot-fish, azure and slim,
How alert in attendance be.
5   From his **saw-pit** of mouth, from his **charnel** of maw
They have nothing of harm to dread,
But liquidly glide on his **ghastly** flank
Or before his Gorgonian head;
Or lurk in the port of **serrated** teeth
10 In white triple **tiers** of glittering gates,
And there find a haven when peril's abroad,
An asylum in jaws of the Fates!
They are friends; and friendly they guide him to prey,
Yet never partake of the treat—
15 Eyes and brains to the dotard lethargic and dull,
Pale **ravener** of horrible meat.

                        Herman Melville

Word cloud

charnel   saw-pit
ghastly   serrated
ravener   tiers

Understanding

1. Why is the pilot fish a friend of the shark?
2. What else does the poem tell you about the pilot fish?
3. In what ways does the writer portray the shark?
4. What makes you think that the writer had experience of the sea? Does this make the poem better? Why?
5. Imagine that you see a Maldive shark at close quarters. Write in your diary your account of what you saw.

Word builder

Pay close attention to the vocabulary of the poem because it gives a very accurate picture of sea life.

Why does Melville use the word 'tiers' for the shark's teeth?

Explain how the other words in the Word cloud give us a more real picture of the shark.

Glossary

phlegmatical not easily excited or worried

sot idiot

maw stomach of a hungry animal

Gorgonian in myths, you turned to stone if you looked at a Gorgon, so 'terrible'

dotard silly old person

1. A long time ago, people used to confuse the word 'ghastly' with 'ghostly'. What do you imagine when you see the word 'ghastly'? The word 'aghast' means 'terrified' – so how does this word make you feel about the shark?

2. 'Ravenous' means eating hungrily, with the idea of tearing your meal apart. How does Melville's word 'ravener' add to what you feel about this shark?

3. You know about the danger of sharks to humans when they bite. How does 'serrated' explain why a shark attack is so terrible?

4. Why does Melville use 'charnel' to describe the shark's stomach? Charnels are usually found in burial grounds, not inside animals.

5. What does the image of a saw-pit suggest about the size of the shark's mouth and teeth?

Developing your language – poetic imagery

1. Use the words of the poem to discuss why this cartoon of a shark isn't like the one you have read about. List the ways in which it is different.

2. Draw your own cartoon of the Maldive shark. You can draw it from any angle or distance.

3. Look further at the words Melville uses to describe the shark's teeth:

   Or lurk in the port of serrated teeth

   In white triple tiers of glittering gates

   Why does he describe them as white, glittering gates and in what way are they a port? How does 'haven' suggest the same thing?

4. Look at the way the pilot fish are described:

   The sleek little pilot fish, azure and slim… liquidly glide.

   Why are they called pilot fish? What do 'sleek', 'azure', 'slim', 'liquidly' and 'glide' add to the picture of the fish?

5. Now you have had a chance to study the poem, what do you think of it? Write a paragraph saying why you do or don't enjoy it.

Poetic predators

💬 Expressing preferences and giving your opinions

In the old days, you weren't encouraged to give your opinions – only the right answer. This exercise will make you realise that there isn't always a right answer.

The Great Poetry Competition

There are four finalists in the Great Poetry Competition: 'To the snake', 'Medallion', 'The Tyger' and 'The Maldive Shark'.

Work together. Imagine you are the judges and you have to choose which is first, second, third and fourth. Discuss your reasons.

Start with the fourth place and move up. You will probably disagree on some points and you will have to discuss these and reach a compromise. Remember that in the end you must express a preference and choose a winner.

1. Discuss what the poem is about and what happens in it. You could say:

   I was very interested in this poem because I had never thought about the animal in the way in which the writer presents it. It was unusual and it grabbed my attention.

   OR

   This poem really made me use my imagination – it was so realistic that I felt quite excited / scared.

2. Talk about the language of the poem. You could say:

   The writer used several words that painted such a realistic picture of the animal that I could really imagine it.

   (Give examples of words and phrases.)

   OR

   My favourite line in the poem was … because …

   AND

   You can talk about any alliteration, images, onomatopoeia, rhymes or the shape of the poem that you enjoyed. (Quote examples and explain what they mean to you and why you like them.)

3. Explain why you have chosen the poem that you think is the winner and why it is better than the others. If you found it difficult to choose between two of them, say so – and why.

Writing about your preferences and opinions

You have just discussed some of your own opinions. Now you have the chance to write about some more of them.

In the old days you weren't allowed to write 'I' so you couldn't give your own opinions.

It was like being gagged!

Nowadays it isn't like that, but you must be responsible. Your opinions must be sensible and thoughtful. Good writers mind their language and are careful not to be rude to people.

1. Explain why these opinions are NOT responsible:

    a *I hate this poem / my Chinese lesson / school – it's just boring!!!*

    b *My teacher is horrid. She won't let me text my best friend during the lesson.*

    c *I don't like scallops – I've never tried them.*

    d *Don't get me started on people who walk slowly.*

2. Write three or four sentences starting with these words:

    a *In my opinion…*

    b *I think that…*

    c *For me, there are advantages and disadvantages about…*

3. Now write a page on whether school uniform is a good idea.

    Think of advantages such as: everyone looks the same and no one shows off; you don't have to think what to wear; people recognise you as belonging to your school.

    Disadvantages are: most school uniform looks unfashionable; it's uncomfortable – itchy or too hot; it's expensive and I keep growing out of it; it stops you expressing yourself.

    You may have other ideas. Decide which side you are on and try to persuade other people to agree with you by what you write.

Expressing preferences

Write a page about your favourite and your least favourite day out, structuring your writing by using some of these reasons: the place; the journey; who you're with; what you do there; how you feel when you get home.

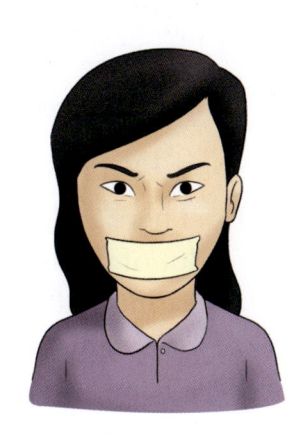

Poetic predators

What is your opinion?

You've had practice in giving your own, sensible opinions. Now here is a chance to respond to someone else's opinions.

Read this text carefully and note down the writer's opinions about the conservation of tigers.

Don't save the tigers

by Vikram Ghosh

1 There's a lot of nonsense talked about spending a lot of money to make sure tigers do not become extinct. After all, animals do become extinct every now and again. It is part of a natural process after
5 all and tigers are no exception. You can spend a whole lot of money that could be spent on world poverty for example, in protecting these animals which let's face it, cause a good deal of pain to villagers in areas where they live. How would you
10 like your animals killed and even your friends and relatives? It's not as if many of you will ever see a tiger in the wild. There are plenty of films on television and cameras can get close up, closer than you would dare. If you really want to see
15 these smelly animals live, then go to a zoo. That's just as good. Seeing a tiger is no great deal; they are just a big cat, and there are plenty of those about.

Start a list of the writer's opinions. The first two are done for you and you can complete the others.

1. Extinction is part of the natural process.
2. You could spend the money put aside for conservation on better things.
3. Tigers can kill _____
4. Few of you will ever see _____
5. You get closer to a tiger by watching _____
6. If you must see them live, go _____
7. Tigers are nothing more than _____

Task

Write a letter to Vikram Ghosh arguing that tigers should be protected and disagreeing with his views.

In your letter you are to comment on what the writer says and argue against him. Decide which of his views you disagree with most, and explain why. Don't write about the topic, just his views.

It is a good idea to do some research to help you to answer what Vikram Ghosh says. If you type 'World Wildlife Fund Tiger' or 'Tiger Conservation' into your search engine, you will find a lot of information. If you use this in your answer, make sure it helps to answer his opinions.

How do I start?

Your first paragraph is an introduction. It gives your reaction to the text as a whole and makes your position clear. This is how you might begin:

Dear Vikram Ghosh

I recently read an article you wrote about the conservation of tigers. I think that the tiger is a specially beautiful animal and an important part of the food chain, and I would be very sad if this important species were to die out and our children would no longer have the chance to see them in the wild.

How do I go on?

It is a good idea to start a paragraph by quoting what Vikram Ghosh says.

In your article you say 'It is part of a natural process after all and tigers are no exception.' I agree that extinction is often a part of a natural process, but in this case it is different because…

You could also start a paragraph by saying:

My chief reason for disagreeing with you is…

How do I finish?

You could begin your final paragraph:

To sum up my objections to your article…

Now write your answer to the task. You do not need to respond to all Vikram Ghosh's views.

Poetic predators

Sample answers for discussion

Read these responses to Vikram Ghosh's article.

Letter 1

Dear Vikram Ghosh

I read your silly article. I think you're talking a lot of tosh. What do you mean how would you like your friends and relatives killed? Serve them right for living near the tigers. What do they expect?

And another thing I didn't like it when you said about television. My TV hasn't got good reception so I can't see the programmes clearly, so what's the point of that?

I also read that tigers were smelly animals but I don't agree. They are big cats, so they spend a lot of time keeping clean.

I bet you don't really know much about tigers so what you say is silly.

Signed

Absit.

Letter 2

Dear Vikram Ghosh

I read your article about conservation of tigers and while I could understand your reasons, I thought the whole thing was very biased. In our modern global village, we know when an important species is in danger of extinction and we can do something about it, so extinction is not necessarily 'the natural order of things'. I find this argument illogical, yet it is fundamental to your whole article.

You say that 'not many of you will see a tiger in the wild'. That is true, but it is not a point against conservation. Not many of us will fly to the moon but there are still space flights and they are expensive too. The tiger holds a vital place in the hierarchy of animals, and the food chain. It is just as illogical to compare spending money on conservation with relieving world poverty. They are different things and have no relation to each other.

The thought of seeing tigers in zoos does not appeal to me. I am sure that tigers in the wild are not smelly. Cages or muddy enclosures are not good environments for these noble animals. No wonder they look tired and are smelly.

You take the easy way out. I would rather work to guarantee the tiger's safety.

Yours sincerely

Anita Allee

Letter 3

Dear Vikram Ghosh

Did you know that poachers are killing tigers as I write and that you can contribute to a fund to adopt a tiger? If you did you would feel closer to the tiger population even if you never saw a wild one.

I don't accept your idea about tigers being 'just a big cat'. Have you ever looked closely at a tiger's face and seen those lovely colours? No cat's like that.

I half agree with your opinion about watching tigers on TV. With a big screen it is exciting. However, it would be better in proper 3D so that tigers could leap at you. Anyway, producers decide what you see.

Then there is your point about spending a lot of money. We don't actually spend much on tigers and we spend far more on world poverty.

Perhaps we should spend some money helping poor villagers whose animals and relatives get attacked by tigers. I see your point, but it doesn't happen to most of us, probably just in India, so that isn't a reason for letting them get extinct.

Yours sincerely

Alfredo

- Discuss the answers in groups.
- Put them in order: best, less good and least good. How did you decide on the order?
- Which shows the best understanding of the article?
- Which reasons in each answer are good and which are less good?
- There are no errors in the writing, but which is written in the best language and the best order?

8 People and places

Explore
- A village in Trinidad
- Nomadic life in the Gobi Desert

Create
- A story that starts with describing a character
- A presentation about where you live and the people around you

Engage
- With the ambitions of a father for his son
- With the lifestyles of people different from you

Collaborate
- In group discussions about world issues: water and poverty
- To learn about how writers present character

In this unit you will:

Reflect
- On the roles you can take in a discussion
- On the importance of a good water supply

Where would you like to live if you had the chance?

"Smile at strangers and you just might change a life."
Steve Maraboli

"Kindness is the language which the deaf can hear and the blind can see."
Mark Twain

"Perhaps travel cannot prevent bigotry, but by demonstrating that all peoples cry, laugh, eat, worry and die, it can introduce the idea that if we try to understand each other, we may even become friends."
Maya Angelou

Thinking time

1. Think about what you see in the two pictures. What would it be like to live in those places? Which would you prefer?
2. What did Mark Twain mean when he said that kindness was 'the language which the deaf can hear and the blind can see'? Why do you think kindness is important?
3. What does Maya Angelou mean by 'bigotry'? How far does what she says defeat bigotry?

Speaking and listening – a presentation

Prepare a presentation about the place where you live and the people that live with you. Think about the order of your presentation and use photos.

Here are some questions to get you started:

- Where do you live?
- What is your home like?
- Describe some family members.
- Describe the area around where you live.
- Do you like living there? Where would you prefer to live when you grow up?

You could use some notes, or just use keywords to remind you what to say next.

Look at your audience and don't forget to smile.

Let them ask questions at the end.

How may a presentation on your school be different? Explain your answer.

People and places

📖 A drink of water

1   The time when the rains didn't come for three months and the sun was a yellow **furnace** in the sky was known as the Great Drought in Trinidad. It happened when everyone was expecting the sky to burst open with rain to fill the dry streams and water the **parched** earth.

5   But each day was the same; the sun rose early in a blue sky, and all day long the farmers lifted their eyes, wondering what had happened. (…) They rested on their hoes and forks and wrung perspiration from their clothes, seeing no hope in labour, terrified by the thought that if no rain fell soon they would lose their crops
10 and livestock and face starvation and death.

In the tiny village of Las Lomas, out in his vegetable garden, Manko licked dry lips and passed a wet sleeve over his dripping face. Somewhere in the field a cow mooed mournfully, sniffing around for a bit of green in the **cracked** earth. The field was a **desolation** of
15 drought. The trees were naked and barks peeled off trunks as if they were diseased. When the wind blew, it was heavy and unrelieving, as if the heat had taken all the spirit out of it. But Manko still opened his shirt and turned his chest to it when it passed.

He was a big man, grown brown and burnt from years of working
20 on the land. His arms were bent and he had a crouching position even when he stood upright. When he laughed he showed more tobacco stain than teeth.

But Manko had not laughed for a long time. Bush fires had swept Las Lomas and left the garden plots **charred** and smoking. Cattle
25 were dropping dead in the heat. There was scarcely any water in the village; the river was dry with **scummy** mud. But with patience one could collect a bucket of water. Boiled, with a little sugar to make it drinkable, it had to do.

Sometimes, when the children knew that someone had gone to the
30 river for water, they hung about in the village main road waiting with bottles and calabash shells, and they fell upon the water-carrier as soon as he hove in sight.

'Boil the water first before drinking!' was the warning cry. But even so two children were dead and many more were on the sick list, their
35 parents too poor to seek medical aid in the city twenty miles away.

Word cloud

charred	furnace
cracked	parched
desolation	scummy

Glossary

we poor we are poor

we ain't have no education we don't have any education

we go get old soon and dead we shall soon be old and we'll die

and come a big man in Trinidad and become someone important in Trinidad

Manko sat in the shade of a mango tree and tried to look on the bright side of things. Such a dry season meant that the land would be good for corn seeds when the rains came. He and his wife Rannie had been working hard and saving money in the hope of sending Sunny, their son, to college in the city.

Rannie told Manko: 'We poor, and we ain't have no education, but is all right, we go get old soon and dead, and what we have to think about is the boy. We must let him have plenty learning and come a big man in Trinidad.'

And Manko, proud of his son, used to boast in the evening, when the villagers got together to talk and smoke, that one day Sunny would be a lawyer or a doctor.

But optimism was difficult now. His livestock was dying out, and the market was glutted with yams. He had a great pile in the yard which he could not sell.

Manko took a look at his plot of land and shook his head. There was no sense in working any more today.

from 'A Drink of Water' by Samuel Selvon

Looking closely

Manko speaks using the local way of speaking English although the grammar is incorrect. In a story it is better to write people's speech as they would talk.

People and places

Understanding

1. What did the people of Las Lomas do for a living?
2. Do droughts like this happened often in Trinidad? Explain your answer.
3. How does the description of the trees make it clear how unusually bad the drought is?
4. Explain how the villagers got their water and what they did with it.
5. How do you know that life in Las Lomas was always difficult?
6. At the end of the passage the writer says how the villagers used to get together in the evening to talk and smoke. Imagine that you are Manko, talking to other villagers. The drought is really serious. What would you talk about? In your conversation you could include:
   - the state of the ground and the cattle
   - the serious matter of the water supply
   - when the drought might end
   - what will happen when the drought ends
   - your hopes for your children.

> **Remember**
>
> *Context* means the words in the text near to the ones you are thinking about. The context often changes the meaning of the word in some way.

Word builder

When the writer tells you about the heat in the wind, he calls it 'heavy and unrelieving'. The use of 'heavy' doesn't mean that the wind is physically heavy; he is saying that when the wind blows, the heat seems to push downwards and you have to fight against it.

Look at the words in the Word cloud describing how the earth suffers under terrible heat.

Answer the following questions. In your answers, show how the context changes the meanings of words.

1. How did the garden plots come to be 'charred'? Describe what you would see.
2. What does the writer mean when he talks about the 'cracked earth'?
3. How does 'parched' personify the earth?

132

4. The writer talks about 'a desolation of drought' – why is this expression effective?

5. Why did the writer say 'scummy mud' and not 'dirty mud'? What effect does 'scummy' add?

Understanding how writers present character

In 'A drink of water' you have only read about one person – or character – called Manko.

You know what Manko looked like – he was big, brown and burnt, had bent arms and back, and his teeth were stained from smoking – but this is his appearance, not his character.

'Character' is what someone is like – for example, you can work out that he was hard-working.

He was also slightly superstitious, as he wondered what had happened to the rain god.

Answer these questions.

1. Give definitions for each of the following words to describe Manko's character. For each one find a quotation from the text to support your answer.

   a a devoted father

   b optimistic even when times were bad

   c sociable

   d defiant

   e liked to laugh a lot

2. Imagine you are Sunny, Manko's son. You have become a famous doctor and have been asked to write about your early life and what you owe to your father. Write a paragraph about your memories of Manko.

Key concept

Using quotations

When you choose words to describe someone's character the choice is yours, but you should always find a quotation that supports your answer. **Examples:**

- what the writer tells you
- what the person does and says
- what other people say about him or her.

People and places

Life among the animals

1   The people of the Gobi Desert live in one of the most **inhospitable** places on earth. It is a harsh, rocky environment, and it is landlocked. Its **nomadic** inhabitants travel several times a year on camels in search of water. They are accompanied by the animals
5   that they herd: oxen, sheep, and most valuable and beloved of all, their horses. When they arrive at a suitable location, they set up their gers or yurts which can be easily constructed and **dismantled**. These circular tents with their woollen coverings provide coolness in the summer and protection from the extreme cold of the desert
10 winter when the temperature falls drastically to a piercing –40° C. In summer there is warmth and the herders make the most of the pastures, leaving their horses outside to **forage** for themselves.

Every member of a **herder's** family possesses their own horse – in fact the population is smaller than the number of horses.
15 Mongolians **process** mares' milk into airag, the national beverage, although they mainly use horses for riding, at which they are extremely accomplished. They are famous for horse racing for they gallop with great velocity. Women also have extensive knowledge of **horsemanship**. They say, 'A Mongolian
20 without a horse is like a bird without wings.'

So if you want to visit the Gobi Desert, and love horses, you will be welcomed with open arms. These people are known for their hospitality and a proverb says, 'Happy is the one who has guests; merry is the home that boasts a tethering rail with
25 many visitors' horses.'

Word cloud

dismantled
forage
herder
horsemanship
inhospitable
nomadic
process

Glossary

gers, yurts a special type of tent

airag a light drink made from mares' milk, slightly sour to the taste.

velocity speed in a certain direction

with open arms with great friendship; pleased to see you

tethering rail a bar for tying your horse to while you are absent

Understanding

Answer these questions.

1. What do the inhabitants of the Gobi Desert do for a living?
2. How do they travel about?
3. Explain how the yurts protect the herders and their families from the weather.
4. In what way do the women seem to be equal to the men?
5. Explain the proverb, 'A Mongolian without a horse is like a bird without wings.'
6. How would you prepare for a trip to this community?

Developing your language – words about a lifestyle

Someone's way of life is their lifestyle. Manko's lifestyle was one of poverty and back-breaking hard work for little reward.

Each of the words in the Word cloud hints at something that Mongolian nomads spend their time doing – that helps make up their lifestyle.

'Dismantled' tells you that their homes are made to be taken apart. Although they are comfortable and made with strong circular wooden frames, this word reminds you that they do not stay in the same place for long.

Answer the following questions.

1. The people described in the extract are said to be 'herders' and to live a 'nomadic' life. Explain what this tells you about their lifestyle.

2. What hints do the words 'horsemanship' and 'forage' tell you about the interests of these nomads?

3. What hint does 'process' give you about the herders' way of life?

Word builder

Lifestyles – work and play

Write two paragraphs.

Paragraph 1

- How much of my time I spend working
- What I do
- Who I work with
- Whether I think the time I spend working is worthwhile

Paragraph 2

- What I do for recreation and play
- My favourite activities
- Who I share my activities with
- Which is more important to me, work or play?

People and places

Compound sentences

You know about simple sentences, for example: *Every member of a herder's family possesses their own horse.*

You also know about coordinated sentences, for example: *It is a harsh, rocky environment, and it is landlocked.*

Discuss how this sentence is different.

> When they arrive at a suitable location, they set up their gers or yurts which can be easily constructed and dismantled.

The main sentence (or clause) is: *They set up their gers or yurts.*

When they arrive at a suitable location tells you the time when they set up their tents.

Which can be easily constructed or dismantled tells you about the tents.

Remember

A *simple sentence* has one verb and one subject. Two sentences joined together by 'and', 'but' and 'so' are *coordinated sentences*.

Answer the questions about this compound sentence:

> Mongolians process mares' milk into airag, the national beverage, although they use horses mainly for riding, at which they are extremely accomplished.

1. How many verbs can you count in the compound sentence?
2. Which is the main clause and how do you know?
3. What word does 'at which' tell you about?
4. What do you think 'although' means?

Which of these are main clauses and which are subordinate?

1. You will be welcomed with open arms
2. That they herd
3. If you want to visit the Gobi Desert
4. The people of the Gobi Desert live in one of the most inhospitable places on earth

Remember

A *main clause* is the most important part of a compound sentence and is complete in itself. A *subordinate clause* tells you about a word in the main clause and does not make sense by itself.

Conjunctions

Use the right conjunction for each gap. Then read the sentence to make sure it makes sense.

1. _____ I first read about the nomads of the Gobi Desert, they seemed to me to be tough people _____ they could survive such winter cold.
2. The nomads would not be able to survive _____ it was not for three things _____ are their tents, their animals and warm summers.
3. The Gobi Desert is an unusual place _____ I might like to go _____, of course, it was in mid-winter.

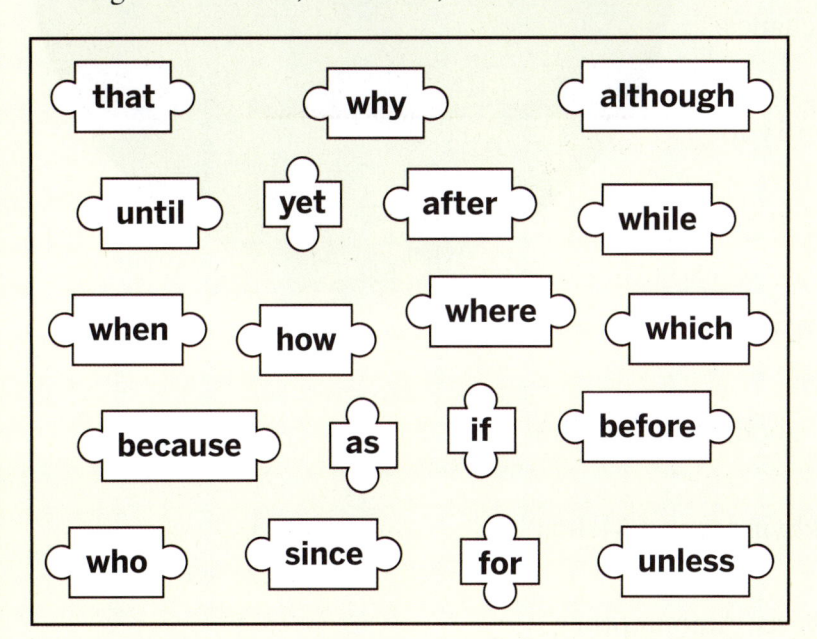

that · why · although · until · yet · after · while · when · how · where · which · because · as · if · before · who · since · for · unless

Remember

Conjunctions are used to link sentences together. Examples: when, where, why, who, which, if, although, because, for, since, as, after, before, how, that, unless, until, while, yet

Tip

There are many ways of building sentences – making compound sentences is only one of them. Try to vary the length and types of your sentences in writing. Be care with careless, overlong sentences.

Practice makes perfect

Use the list of conjunctions to make some compound sentences of your own. Each one should have a main clause and two subordinate clauses – three verbs in all.

Danger ahead!

What is wrong with the following sentence? Explain your answer and write down an improved version.

> I'm just back from Mongolia and I feel ill but I don't know why because I was careful what I had whenever it was mealtime when they gave you so much that I couldn't finish unless it was something I liked which wasn't often so they must've thought I was fussy but I'm not well because maybe it was something I ate, but I don't know.

People and places

Living in different countries

You are going to hear a group discussion about living in different countries. The teacher, Miss Favoro, has organized it but does not take part. You will hear two girls, Sukhvinder and Melina, and two boys, Gopal and Angelo.

Before you listen to this extract, think about the contribution each student could make to the discussion. What could they think about the following statements?

1. Where you are born is just a matter of chance.
2. Water is important to everyone's lives.
3. Some people go to live in another country to hope for a better life.

Understanding

1. What job did Miss Favoro give to Sukhvinder?
2. Why did she want Gopal to keep notes?
3. Why did Melina use the word 'lottery' about the place you are born in?
4. Explain the disagreement between Sukhvinder and Melina about living in Mongolia.
5. The students talk quite a lot about poverty. Among other things, Sukhvinder says that poverty is relative. What do you understand by the word 'poverty'?

Understanding how a group works

> Miss Favoro said I was the chair. I keep the discussion in order and, when people have had their say, I move the discussion on. Everyone must have a chance to say something. I sometimes make a summary of what has been said.

I had to keep notes and make a record of the discussion so we could report back. My job was to listen, and I needed to be a quick writer – which I wasn't.

They need Angelo and me to make intelligent ideas and explanations. I listen to the others and I agree or disagree with them.

I was very helpful when Melina didn't know 'dehydrate' and I finished her sentence for her. I think I had the best ideas.

You are Miss Favoro. You have heard the recording of the discussion. What would you say to each of the four students about the part they played in the discussion?

Speaking and listening – group discussions

Now you have thought about the different parts people play in discussions, try the following, based on what you heard in the recording.

1. **a** Discuss the importance of water to people all over the world.
   b Why we need it.
   c What happens when there is a drought. Places where there is a problem in getting enough water.
   d How some disasters are caused by too much of it.
2. Discuss what you understand by poverty and why it is a world problem. Make a short list of things you can discuss.

Tip

Listen carefully to other people when sharing ideas in a group discussion. If you take turns without interrupting, your group discussion will be much better!

People and places

How do I start a story? Using a character

You've probably wondered how to start a story. One way is to present a character and let your story grow out of your description.

This is the beginning of a story called 'The Ostler'. In the old days an ostler was the person who looked after travellers' horses when they stayed at an inn overnight.

The sleeping man

1   I find an old man, fast asleep, in one of the stalls of the stable. It is midday, and rather a strange time for an **ostler** to devote to sleep. Something **curious**, too, about the man's face. A **withered woebegone** face. The eyebrows painfully contracted; the mouth
5   fast set, and drawn down at the corners; the **hollow** cheeks sadly, and, as I cannot help **fancying, prematurely** wrinkled; the **scanty, grizzled** hair, telling weakly its own tale of some past **sorrow** or suffering. How fast he draws his breath, too, for a man asleep! He is talking in his sleep.
10 'Wake up!' I hear him say, in a quick whisper through his fast-clenched teeth. 'Wake up there! Murder!'

From *The Ostler* by Wilkie Collins

Word cloud

curious	prematurely
fancying	scanty
grizzled	sorrow
hollow	withered
ostler	woebegone

Talk about this – what's interesting about this person? Does it suggest more to you than just describing what he looked like? How do you think the story might go on (and even finish?)

Here are some more characters who might start off a story…

140

Using vocabulary to create characters

1. Write the beginning of a story by describing a character. You can use an idea from one of the pictures, choose a picture of your own, or create a character from your own imagination.

- **Appearance** – What does your character look like?
- **Clothes** – What is the character wearing?
- **Characteristics** – What can you tell about them from their appearance?
- **Speech** – Does the character say anything and in what tone of voice?
- **Place** – Where does your story take place?

Decide who is telling the story – you or somebody else?

How will you finish your description to lead on to what happens in the story?

You could start your description like this:

> As I turned the corner of the deserted side street, I was suddenly confronted by a most disturbing sight.

Or

> My uncle was a jolly person who had a habit of playing practical jokes on me. One day he was sitting at the table without his usual broad smile. His fingers drummed nervously on the table top and I could see that something was the matter.

Or

> There was a knock at the door and when I opened it there was the strangest person I had ever seen.

2. Now you have started your story, stop to think what might happen next and write this down. Remember to make your story grow out of what you have already written and be sure that your character plays a really important part.

People and places

📖 Responding to a narrative

Read this extract and answer the questions that follow.

Questions often ask you to find a quotation to support your answer or to give a word or phrase from the passage that matches a statement. Questions are often about characters and settings. You may have to find examples of devices like personification, alliteration, onomatopoeia, and imagery.

Coming home

1   Landing at the airport had confused Maria. Of course there was no airport when she was a child. She had left the farm when her parents fled the country thirty years ago and had settled
5   a thousand miles away in a place that would protect them. Only now could she pluck up enough courage to return. She wondered where she had found the resolution to do so because she was not an outgoing person, but she needed
10 to take perhaps her only chance to re-discover her roots.

'This way', said a kind voice as she threaded her way through the airport which seemed like a monster to her, ready to swallow her up.

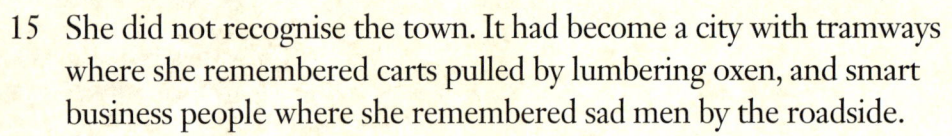

15 She did not recognise the town. It had become a city with tramways where she remembered carts pulled by lumbering oxen, and smart business people where she remembered sad men by the roadside.

Kind people pointed the way to her village when she spoke its name, and Maria set off through tall, smart buildings that once
20 were cornfields. They seemed never-ending, but she knew the farm was near.

Suddenly she saw it. She recognised the weathered, wooden buildings immediately. They appeared the same as ever, ramshackle, but friendly and welcoming. They looked
25 insignificant, hemmed in by the grey faces of the tower blocks of the new university. Maria shed a tear for happy childhood days and entered the farmhouse.

'Yes?' demanded an unfriendly voice. 'What can I do for you?' The woman's face was wrinkled, saddened by time, yet she had

142

the toughness of a farmer's wife. The two women looked at each other for a time, searching for recognition. Then suddenly, the old lady exclaimed with astonishment, 'It can't be! After all these years!' and flung her arms round Maria, weeping with amazement. In that moment, Maria recognised her aunt, the brave patriot who had refused to leave her country but stayed to keep the farm alive.

Later, she told her how the university bought the surrounding land, how they offered her money, but how she refused. 'You see, my dear, it was the family tradition. So many generations – I couldn't give it up. It is so good. I never thought to see you again.'

Understanding

1. What sort of person is Maria's aunt? Write one word or phrase in your own words. Give a quotation from the passage to support your answer.
2. Explain in your own words two ways in which the town had changed since Maria was last there.
3. Why did Maria start to cry when she saw the farmhouse?
4. Give two phrases from the passage that show the difference between the university buildings and the farm buildings.
5. Give one example of a simile and one of a metaphor from the passage.

People and places

Sample answers

Here is a selection of sample answers from the exercise on the previous page. **Discuss which you think is the best and why.**

1. What sort of person is Maria's aunt? Write one word or phrase in your own words. Give a quotation from the passage to support your answer.

    i. Unfriendly – quotation: 'demanded an unfriendly voice'

    ii. Unhappy – quotation: 'saddened by time'

    iii. Stubborn – quotation: 'refused to leave her country'; 'offered her money, but she refused'

2. Explain in your own words two ways in which the town had changed since Maria was last there.

    i. Everything looked more modern.

    ii. She did not recognise it.

    iii. There were a lot of businessmen.

    iv. It was much bigger.

    > **Tip**
    > Remember that the question asked about change.

3. Why did Maria start to cry when she saw the farmhouse?

    i. Maria shed a tear for happy childhood days.

    ii. Seeing the farmhouse suddenly brought happy memories back to her.

    iii. She wanted to be a child again.

4. Give two phrases from the passage that show the difference between the university buildings and the farm buildings.

    i. 'Maria set off through tall, smart buildings that once were cornfields.'

    ii. 'The same as ever, ramshackle…'

    iii. 'The grey faces of the tower blocks'

    iv. 'They looked insignificant'

    > **Tip**
    > Be careful to read the question! It asked for the difference.

5. Give one example of a simile and one of a metaphor from the passage.

    i. 'Like a monster' is a simile

    ii. 'The same as ever' is a simile.

    iii. 'Lumbering' is a metaphor.

    iv. 'Threaded' is a metaphor.

Teacher commentary

1. The first two answers are only slightly true. She was only unfriendly for a moment, and although her face showed unhappiness, there is no evidence that she was more unhappy than anything else. There is a lot of evidence that she would not give up easily and that she stuck by her tradition and her pride.

2. Answer ii might be the result of changes, but it does not tell you what they are and it is not in 'own words'. There could be plenty of businessmen but that is a fact, not a change. Being more modern and being much bigger are both comparatives and therefore express change.

3. Answer i: You were not asked for a quotation so answer in your own words to show you understand what you read. Answer iii is partly true but it is not the full answer – it was seeing the farmhouse and remembering that made her cry.

4. Read the question carefully and look for two quotations that go together to show a difference. The first two do this by contrasting 'smart' with 'ramshackle'. The other pair only suggest a colour and the small size of the farmhouse buildings.

5. 'Like a monster' is a good simile because it compares one thing with another. 'The same as ever' doesn't make a comparison although it uses 'as'. 'Lumbering' is a difficult word because it means several things, but here it is a meaning and not a borrowed comparison. However, 'threaded' is what you do with a needle and cotton and it is used here to describe how Maria made her way through the crowds, looking for the gaps.

> **Tip**
>
> Before you answer the questions, make sure you have understood the whole story.
>
> Read the questions very carefully.
>
> Go back to the context to find the best answer.
>
> Use your own words unless you are asked for a quotation.

9 Challenge!

In this unit you will:

Explore
- different texts on the topic of challenge
- why teamwork is important

Create
- a story about a challenge
- a list of principles for successful group work

Engage
- with a story about two children lost in the desert
- with why challenges are important for young people

Collaborate
- to tackle a group challenge
- to revise your reading skills

Reflect
- on your strengths and areas for development in English
- on how language is used to convey meaning

"There are no negatives in life, only challenges to overcome that will make you stronger."
Eric Bates

"Those who overcome great challenges will be changed, and often in unexpected ways."
Steve Goodier

"Life is either a daring adventure or nothing."
Helen Keller

9

Thinking time

1. Note down some of the associations word 'challenge' has for you. The quotations and images opposite may help.

   Compare your ideas with a partner.

2. Can you think of some examples of both positive and negative challenges? Discuss with a partner some of the words you might associate with each.

This unit will explore the theme of challenge but also give you the opportunity to reflect on your strengths and areas for development as a learner.

Speaking and listening

On your own, think about what you are good at and which English skills you need to develop further. You should think about your skills in:

- Speaking and listening
- Reading
- Writing.

Now discuss this in small groups, suggesting ways to help each other develop these skills.

Challenge!

🎧 A new year, a new start

Key skills for revision

- Listening carefully
- Working in a group
- Evaluating your own and others' use of language

Listen to this talk from a head teacher to the students in her school at the beginning of a school year. After you hear the talk for the first time, jot down the three main ideas you have taken from it.

Share these with a partner. Are their ideas the same or different?

When you hear it for the second time, capture the key points in six bullet points.

It is a good idea when you listen to a speech or a conversation to try to identify the main ideas or points immediately, before you forget them. It can be difficult to separate the main ideas from the supporting detail. One way is to imagine you are in a lift and someone asks you to summarise what you have just heard by the time you reach the next floor. This can help you to focus on the most important aspects of what you have heard. (N.B. This works when you are reading a text too!)

Word cloud

aspirations
critical
execute
prototypes

Glossary

marshmallow a light, very soft, chewy cylindrical sweet

Understanding

1. What are the three main points the head teacher wants to make to her students?
2. Explain in your own words what the 'marshmallow challenge' is.

148

3. Identify two reasons why learning to work as a team is important.
4. Identify two ways you know this is spoken text.
5. Did you agree with the ideas in this speech? Do you think the head teacher is right?

Word builder

1. Look at the words in the Word cloud: 'aspirations', 'critical', 'execute' and 'protype' and see if you can work out what each of them means in context. It is often possible to puzzle out what words mean when you think about them in the context of a text. Here is each of them in context:

    'encourage you to have high aspirations for yourself'

    'It's no good coming up with an idea and then letting someone else execute it'

    'they build lots of prototypes – they try lots of different approaches out –'

    'being able to work in a team is critical'

2. If you can't work out what these words mean, look them up in a dictionary and then try to rewrite each sentence using your own words.

Homonyms

'Critical and 'execute' have more than one meaning. Do you know what the different meanings are? Words like these are called *homonyms*.

Here are some more examples. When you are reading you have to be aware of which meaning a writer intends when he or she is writing. Sometimes it depends on which part of speech a word is being used as:

bank	examine	quarry
cast	express	refuse
cataract	palm	rock
entrance	pupil	scrap

Look at these words and discuss the different meanings they can have.

> **Tip**
> Watch out for words with more than one meaning. They can be very confusing.

> **Tip**
> Some homonyms are pronounced differently and some can have more than two meanings!

> **Challenge!**

Developing your language

The head teacher uses language and other techniques to encourage her students to listen carefully and remember.

Match each of the techniques below to the correct example from the head teacher's speech. Before you start, check that you are clear what each of the techniques is.

first person plural	the first day is like a new page in a work book
rhetorical question	isn't it?
rule of three	just look around at your friends and peers
colloquial language	What's the secret of success?
similes	it's young kids
direct address to the audience	sit back and kick their heels
first person singular	it's called having a 'growth mindset'
tag questions	it's important to me
idioms	another test, another homework, another piece of work
technical language	at this school we are all part of the same team

Now think about the effect of each of these techniques on the intended audience.

💬 Speaking and listening

Plan a challenge, like the 'marshmallow challenge', for a group of students, to help them develop and test team work. Then swap challenges and take it in turns to carry out each challenge.

Discuss which of the following are common errors in group tasks.

- It's best if one person takes charge and does most of the talking.
- It's important to check what others in the group are thinking and that everyone is happy with decisions.
- You just have to wait your turn to say something.
- Sometimes, just one contribution can make a difference.
- I don't say anything because other people don't ask me.

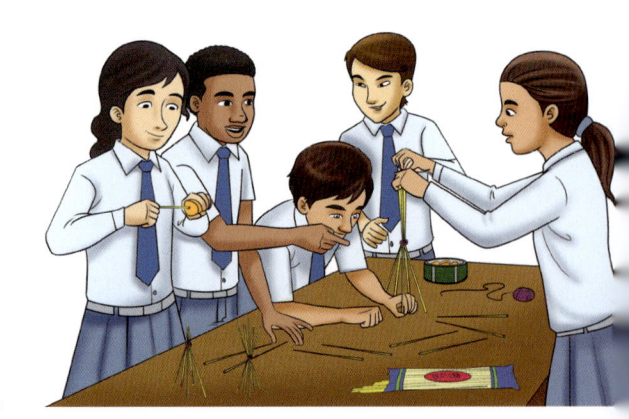

Each team should observe the other team. At the end, give feedback to the students who carried out your challenge on how well they worked as a team. You could use the traffic light system below. Try to make sure your feedback is constructive and identify particular ways of speaking that helped to move group work forward effectively.

Level	Criteria
Green	Everyone contributed to the discussion, listened to each other and tried to build on others' contributions. They managed to complete the challenge effectively and found ways to resolve differences. They kept on task throughout and everyone was fully engaged in completing the task, focusing on reaching a conclusion.
Amber	Almost everyone contributed to the discussion and people tried to listen to each other, though they didn't always build on what other people were saying. They managed to complete the challenge, though it didn't always go smoothly. They were on task for most of the time and although some people said more than others, the whole group was engaged with the task.
Red	Most people tried to contribute to the discussion but didn't always listen to each other. They managed to do the challenge – but not complete it very effectively – and they sometimes went off task and talked about other things. One or more people tended to dominate the discussion and not everyone was engaged with the task.

Tip

Before you carry out your challenge, remind yourselves what makes for good group work. It can be helpful to write these points on a large sheet of paper, to keep you focused.

Challenge!

📖 **Reading – Walkabout**

Key skills for revision
- Making inferences
- Using supporting quotations
- Exploring the use of language

Read this extract from a novel called *Walkabout*. Peter and Mary are on their way to visit their uncle in Adelaide, Australia. Their plane has crashed and they find themselves alone and stranded in the Australian bush. Mary is 14 and Peter is 6.

Walkabout

1   'I'm hungry,' He announced cheerfully. 'What can we eat?'

'There's barley sugar in your pocket.'

He pulled out the sticky fragment.

5   'It's not much.'

He broke it and dutifully offered her half. But she shook her head.

'It's all right,' she said. 'I've had mine.'

She watched him as, cheeks bulging, hands in pockets, he went
10   **strolling** down by the creek. Thank heavens he didn't seem to be worried: not yet. Whatever happened he must never realize how worried she was; must never lose faith in her ability to look after him.

She watched him exploring their strange surroundings; watched him drop flat on his stomach and knew he was Davy Crockett,
15   reconnoitring a new frontier. He wriggled along in the sand, cautiously **peering** across to the farther bank of the stream. Suddenly he leapt to his feet, clutched the seat of his trousers and gave an almighty yell of anguish. Again and again he **yelled**, as again and again red-hot needles of pain shot through his **squirming** body.

20   Mary tumbled and slithered down the rocks; rushed to his aid. For a second she couldn't think what had happened; then she too felt the red-hot needle of pain, and looking down saw their assailants. Ants. Jumping ants. Three-quarters of an inch long, forty per cent jaw and forty per cent powerful grass-hop-perish
25   legs. She saw their method of attack at once; saw how they hunched themselves up, then catapulted through the air – often

152

several feet – on to their prey. She half-dragged, half-carried Peter away, at the same time hauling off his trousers.

'It's all right,' she gasped. 'They're only ants. Look. Hanging on to your trousers. Biting away as if you're still inside.'

His **wailing** stopped; he looked at his discarded shorts. It was true. The ants were still there; their wispy antennae weaving from side to side like the arms of so many punch-drunk boxers; their mandibles were open wide, eager to bite again. But they weren't given the chance. With a shout of rage Peter **elbowed** his sister aside and started to jump on the shorts; his feet **thudded** into the denim, pounding and crushing, **pulverizing** the ants to death. Or so he thought.

Mary stood aside; relieved; half-amused at the violence of his revenge. She had seen the ants sneaking clear of the shorts. But she said nothing. Not until his pounding feet threatened to damage his trousers. Then she reached for his hand.

'O.K., Peter. They're all dead now.'

She helped him on with his shorts.

He started to whimper then; the pain of the bites touching off a host of half-formed fears. Mary's arms went round him. He felt small and shivery and thin; she could feel his heart thudding between his ribs.

'It's all right, Pete, she whispered. I won't let them bite you again.'

His sobs died; but only momentarily. Then they started again.

'What is it, Pete?'

'I don't like this place.'

Now it's coming, she thought. It's coming, and there's nothing I can do about it.

'I don't like it here, Mary. I wanna go home.'

'But we can't go home, Peter. We've got nothing to cross the sea in.'

'Then let's go to Uncle Keith. In Adelaide.'

She was surprised how much he'd remembered. Their plane had been bound for Adelaide.

'All right,' she said slowly. 'I'll take you to Uncle Keith.'

Instantly his sobbing stopped.

'When? Now?'

'Yes,' she said, 'now. We'll start to walk to Adelaide.'

from *Walkabout* by James Vance Marshall

Word cloud

elbowed
peering
pulverizing
squirming
strolling
thudded
wailing
yelled

Glossary

barley sugar a sweet made of boiled sugar

Davy Crockett 19th-century American folk hero

mandibles parts of an insect's mouth used to grab and crush food

Looking closely

'Reconnoitring' means making an observation of a place in a military way. It comes from the Latin word 'recognoscere' which means to know again (which is also the origin of the word 'recognise') and the old French word 'reconnoitre'. It is appropriate here because in the next part of the story, Peter is attacked by an army of ants!

Challenge!

Key concept

Developing inference

Inference is where you have to read between the lines to work out what is happening or what a character or relationship is like. It isn't necessarily directly stated in the text. When you are making inferences, you often have to give evidence from the text to show where you got your ideas from. If you quote directly, these are called quotations (or quotes for short) and should have inverted commas or quotation marks at the beginning and the end.

Remember

Always use quotation marks at the beginning and end of quotes.

Understanding

Introductory questions – getting to know the text:

1. In the first part of the extract, up to 'look after him', how do Mary and Peter's reactions to the situation they are in differ?

2. Whose point of view is the story told from? How does the writer do this?

And now here is a question which asks you to make inferences:

3. What do you learn about Mary and Peter's relationship?

   Explain in your own words, and support your ideas with quotations from the text.

   Copy out the spidergram opposite to make notes for your answer to this question. Then write your ideas up into a paragraph of writing.

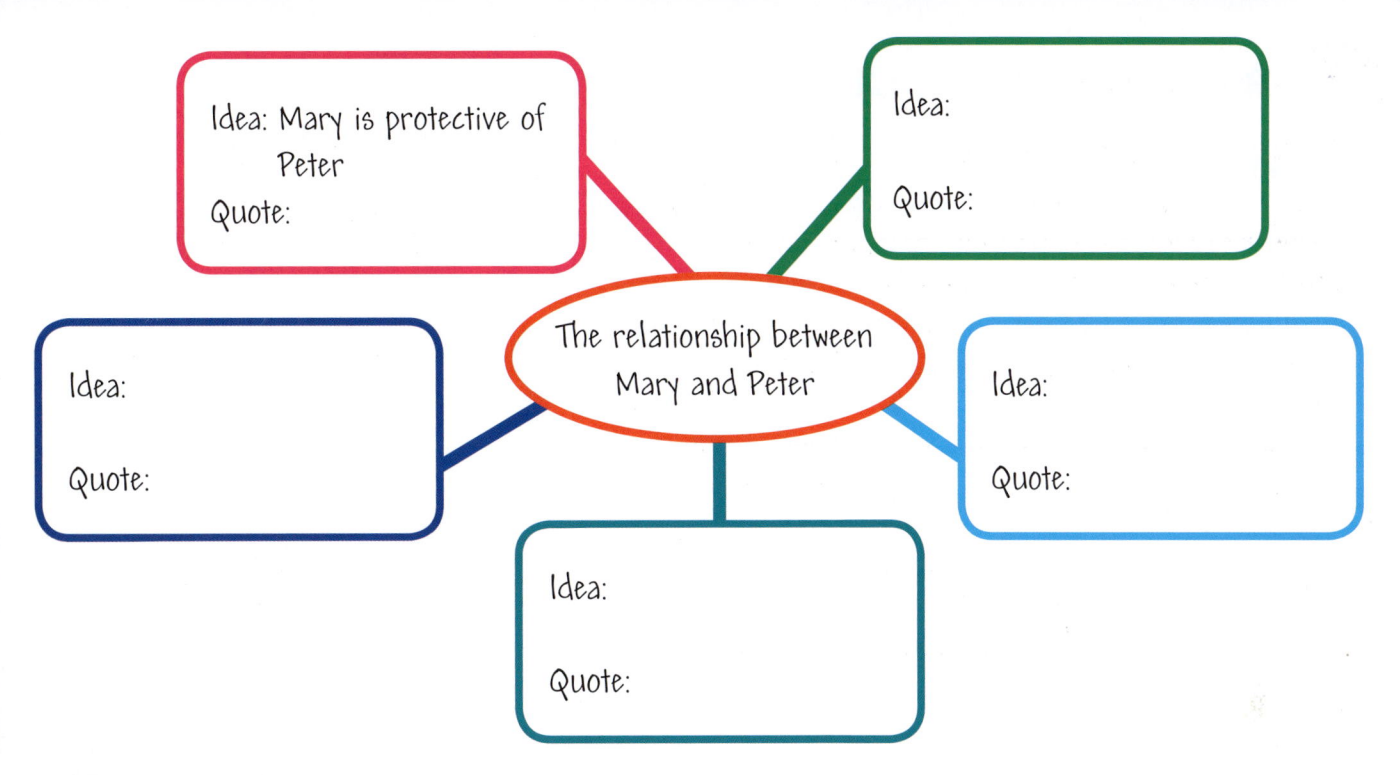

- Idea: Mary is protective of Peter
  Quote:
- Idea:
  Quote:
- Idea:
  Quote:
- Idea:
  Quote:
- Idea:
  Quote:

The relationship between Mary and Peter

Word builder

1. Look at the word 'grass-hop-perish' in the text. Can you work out what it means?
2. What does '–ish' on the end of a word mean? Can you think of occasions when you might want to use words with –ish on the end?

Tip

Don't just paraphrase the meaning of texts. Focus on what the language suggests.

Developing your language – connotations and associations

Look at the verbs used to describe Peter's actions from 'She watched …' to … between his ribs. Some of them are given in the Word cloud on page 153. How do the verbs show Peter's changing mood and feelings here?

Beware of paraphrasing the meaning of a text rather than focusing closely on what the language suggests. Remember to think about the connotations and associations of words – the different ideas and feelings they suggest. Start by identifying the key verbs and then think about the mood or feelings you associate with each one. Some of them may create the same feeling or mood. You could make your notes in two columns, headed 'Verb used to describe Peter' and 'What it suggests about his mood and feelings'.

Challenge!

📖 Reading – World Challenge

Key skills for revision
- summarising main ideas
- identifying features of text types

Read this text from the website of a company which runs adventurous trips or expeditions for schools.

Education through exploration

1 World Challenge is the leading provider of life-changing school expeditions.

From increased confidence and fitness to global awareness and money management, an expedition brings benefits that will have
5 an impact on the rest of your life.

Completing a World Challenge expedition is an educational travel experience that goes on rewarding students, long after they return home. Challengers achieve more than they thought possible by stretching beyond their **comfort zone**, and this sense
10 of accomplishment colours their ongoing view of themselves and their place in the world. They have to **raise the bar** in terms of physical fitness, communication, teamwork and organisation, all highly valuable skills they can draw on in their post-expedition lives. Engaging with another culture during the Project phase
15 brings global awareness that can't be gleaned from books. Students return from their expedition with increased energy and enthusiasm and a sense that if they really apply themselves, there's no limit to what they can do.

With our support, students take ownership of destination
20 research and itinerary planning, fundraising ideas and events, budgeting, preparation, fitness and nutrition. At World Challenge, we believe this build-up programme is as important as the expedition itself, in teaching young people important life skills such as teamwork and money management. Our structured
25 educational programmes, led by experienced staff, teach practical skills and encourage students to take responsibility for themselves and their team.

www.world-challenge.co.uk

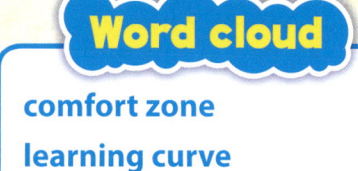

Word cloud
comfort zone
learning curve
raise the bar

Glossary
gleaned gained from

Everything in life is a **learning curve** but my experience in Kenya definitely put me on the path to wanting to find new adventures all over the world and do more interesting and engaging things with my life.

Jamie Maddison, challenger
www.world-challenge.co.uk

Understanding

1. What is the main purpose of this text?
2. Explain the following phrase in your own words: 'goes on rewarding students, long after they return home'.
3. How is the last section different from the rest of the text?

Word builder

The phrases in the Word cloud might be considered as clichés. One way of avoiding clichés is by rewording the phrase. Take one of the phrases above and find two other ways of saying the same thing which are more original.

Developing your language – summarising

Here is an example of a summary question.

Summarise the main benefits for a student of going on a World Challenge expedition.

To answer this question, look at the lists below and then: identify which are the main benefits; add any main benefits that have been left out; sort them into educational and personal benefits.

Take care: not all the benefits are relevant to this text!

- teamwork
- resilience
- enthusiasm
- first aid
- independence
- money management
- taking responsibility
- survival skills
- global awareness
- getting on with people
- understanding the world better
- no limitations

Key concept

Summarising main ideas

Avoid copying out sections of the text unselectively and repeating points.

This skill is about recognising the main ideas in a text and distinguishing them from the supporting details.

Challenge!

✏️ Writing

Key skills for revision:

- planning
- varying sentences
- using correct punctuation
- proofreading

Have a look at the task below, linked to the theme of this unit.

The challenge!

Write a story with this title. It could be about a physical challenge, like learning a new sport or going on an expedition, or it could be another kind of challenge, like dealing with a difficult situation at school or at home. It could be serious or funny. It could be based on your own experience or completely made up.

Remember to think about:

- the setting
- the characters
- the plot

> **⭐ Tip**
>
> It is important to have a plan before you start writing. There are different ways of planning – use the way that suits you best.

Planning

You need to think about:

- the overall structure of your writing (can you sum up what it's about in three sentences?)
- how it's going to begin
- how your ideas are going to be grouped into sections or paragraphs
- how you are going to link your ideas within and across paragraphs
- how it's going to end.

Make sure you plan in paragraphs and that they are part of your thinking right from the start. You could use boxes to represent sections or paragraphs in your writing.

It can be helpful to start by writing the first and last sentences. It is sometimes effective if they are linked or match in some way.

You might also want to think about the semantic field – that is, the kind of words and phrases – you want to use in your writing, and jot down some of them while you are planning.

> In my experience, the most common errors in planning are:
> - not planning at all
> - forgetting that a good ending is just as important as a good opening
> - not checking the plan as you write.

Opening sentences

These should really grab the reader's attention and make them think: I have to read on!

Try writing an opening sentence for each of these writing topics.

- a mystery story
- a personal account of a disastrous day
- a speech arguing that we should look after the environment
- an article about school uniform
- a letter of complaint about a poor meal

Share your opening sentences and decide which are your favourites and why.

Now write a plan for your story.

> **Tip**
> Vary the length and structure of your sentences and don't start them all in the same way.

Varying sentences

Varying sentences means using different sentence lengths, types and structures. You can also think about the order of points in your sentence, starting with a non-finite clause or moving the subject to the end of the sentence. It is often quite effective to start with a short, simple sentence, either to create dramatic effect in a narrative, to introduce the topic in an information text or to state the point of view you want to argue the case for.

Look at the paragraph below. All the sentences are rather short and quite a few begin in the same way. Rewrite this paragraph, making the sentences more varied and therefore more interesting. You can add your own vocabulary and ideas if you want to as well.

> The cave was dark. It was full of shadows. Anya and Zak could only see a little way in. A large boulder jutted out. Anya and Zak stopped and they hesitated and they didn't know what to do. Anya and Zak didn't move. They did not look at each other and they did not say anything. A few seconds passed and it was like the world stood still. Anya coughed and Zak shuffled his feet slightly. The sun slipped behind a cloud. The shadow in the cave reached out. The shadow covered them. Zak shuddered. Anya made a small noise in her throat. She stepped backwards.

> **Tip**
> Don't forget to mark the beginning of a sentence with a capital letter and the end with a full stop, exclamation mark or question mark.

Challenge!

Joining sentences

If you are writing two sentences (or clauses) which are linked in meaning, either use a conjunction like 'when', 'if', 'although', 'because', 'and', etc or use a semicolon. Remember, you should never join sentences with commas. Try to 'hear' each sentence in your head as you write and always check you have marked each one clearly and correctly.

Look at the sentences below and decide which are punctuated correctly and which aren't. Make sure you can explain why a sentence is correct or not and suggest how it can be corrected if it needs it. Remember, there will be more than one way of rewriting a sentence so that it is correct.

1. Sarah summoned up all her determination and threw the discus for the third time; she had done it – she had beaten her personal best!
2. We offer a challenging range of activities for young people, however, all activities are supervised by fully trained staff.
3. Although Li wanted to curl up in his own bed and forget about his piano exam, his mother was determined he should rise to the challenge.
4. She was very nervous before she went on stage she felt absolutely fine once the play started
5. In 2012, 240 people reached the summit of Everest. The highest mountain in the world.

Now write the opening paragraph for your story, making sure you vary your sentences.

Using correct punctuation

Some of the commonest punctuation errors are:
- forgetting apostrophes for omission and possession
- not being sure where to put inverted commas (and other punctuation) in speech
- misusing commas to mark phrases and clauses.

Look back at the skills audit you did at the beginning of this unit and check which aspects of punctuation you need to concentrate on getting right.

Reading your writing aloud will help you to check that your sentence punctuation is correct. If it isn't, you'll find it hard to read your sentence properly. This will also help you with inserting commas to mark phrases and clauses in the right places.

Look at the piece of writing below. Read it through, looking closely at the punctuation. Spot all the errors the writer has made in her punctuation.

What advice would you give to help the writer improve?

When I went to visit my auntie it was a challenge for me, I hadnt been there before and I didnt know what to expect. I kept thinking about what it was going to be like and my imagination was running wild. She would be very strict, she would give me food I didn't like, she would be cross with me. I don't know why I thought my auntie would be like this. I have stayed at my other aunties house lots of times and really enjoyed myself.

My dad took me in the car and all the way there I was feeling nervous despite my dad saying to me, "Youll have a wonderful time with your cousins I know you will".

When we got there my auntie came out to see me and she gave me a big hug. My oldest cousin who is a little older than me was there too and she was smiling and smiling as though she was really pleased to see me.

For dinner we had chicken beans rice and a really nice dessert. Although I felt shy I did manage to join in the conversation and everyone laughed a lot so it was fun. After dinner we went out on bikes and messed around till it was time to go home. We played dares and things like that with my cousins friends and I really enjoyed myself. I forgot that I had been worried about coming to visit, I didn't want to go home!

Now finish writing your story, making sure you keep referring back to your plan and that you pause to read through what you have written as you write.

Challenge!

Proofreading

Always build in time to proofread your work. Here are some guidelines:

- If you can, take a break after you finish writing and before you proofread as this will help you to spot errors more easily.
- Practise proofreading by checking your friends' work for them.
- Be aware of the most important things you are looking for – punctuation of sentences, apostrophes and correct spelling.
- You may need to read through the work more than once, checking for different things separately.
- For your own work, keep a list of errors you know you make – and check particularly for those.
- Don't forget to check titles and subheadings – we often ignore things we assume are correct.
- Professional proofreaders use a ruler to follow the text and make sure they are checking each line and word carefully.

> **Tip**
> Make sure you leave enough time to proofread your work thoroughly.

Watch out for homophones

These are words which sound the same but are spelt differently and have different meanings. They are very easy to confuse, especially if you are writing in a hurry.

Common homophones

accept / except	capital / capitol	stationary / stationery
affect / effect	complement / compliment	there / their / they're
aloud / allowed	here / hear	to / too / two
are / our	it's / its	weather / whether
bear / bare	led / lead	which / witch
brake / break	one / won	you're / your
buy / by	principle / principal	

Go through this list and make sure you know the difference between the words in each pair or three.

If you find some hard to remember, or often get wrong, create a mnemonic to remind you when to use each word.

For example:

*Cars are stationary with an **a** when they are stuck in traffic.*

*Stationery with an **e** refers to pens and pencils.*

162

Non-narrative writing task

Now try a non-narrative writing task, remembering all the key revision points covered in this unit.

> Do you think challenge is important for young people? If so, what kinds of challenges are important?

You could think about:

- why challenges are important for young people
- the different kinds of challenges that young people need to experience
- your own experience of challenges in your life
- challenges you would like to achieve in the future.

Remember to:

- plan your task, thinking about how you are going to start, organise your ideas and end your writing
- vary your sentences to make your writing interesting for the reader
- check to make sure you are using correct punctuation in your writing (keep reading and re-reading to check that what you are writing makes sense)
- proofread your work carefully to pick up any errors you have made. Keep a particular eye out for mistakes you know you make, especially in homophones.

Assessment and reflecting on your learning

Look back at the skills audit you carried out at the beginning of this unit and check whether you have made progress in the skills you wanted to develop further. If you have, well done – you have risen to the challenge! Think too about any areas where you want to keep working to develop your knowledge, skills and understanding.

Write a paragraph about your own learning at the end of this unit. You could write about:

- what you have enjoyed / found interesting
- which of your skills you think have developed and improved
- which of your skills you need to keep working at to develop further.

163

10 Pathways – going places

In this unit you will:

Create
- a compelling advertisement for an amazing location

Explore
- Indonesia, Venezuela, and Venice

Engage
- in choosing a holiday destination

Collaborate
- in deciding why people want to travel

Reflect
- on your reading skills

A change is as good as a rest.

"I have not told the half of what I saw."
Marco Polo, *The Travels of Marco Polo*

"Travelling – it leaves you speechless, then turns you into a storyteller."
Ibn Battuta, a fourteenth century Moroccan traveller and scholar.

Thinking time

1. 'A change is as good as a rest.' This is an old adage, a proverb, but does a change in your normal routine make much difference to how you feel?
2. Do you think travelling and visiting new places can change the way you think?
3. It is easier now than ever before to record what you see when travelling. Do you think taking photographs and putting them onto social media has replaced talking about the places you have seen and the people you have met? Is this a good thing?

Speaking and listening

People have been on the move since the end of the Ice Age when they had to follow the animals they were hunting in order to survive. Nowadays, most people live in one place, but many still make long journeys for work or leisure.

Discuss the following questions with a partner:

- Do you think that travelling is part of human nature?
- Is a school trip the same as a holiday? If not, why not?
- Why do so many people like visiting places they will never live in or return to?
- If you had the opportunity to go anywhere in the world for two weeks, where would you go? Why would you choose that place?

Pathways – going places

📖 **Travel writing**

Travel writing informs and entertains, and it dates back to Ancient Greece and China. In the fourteenth century, Ibn Battuta recorded his travels across the known world from Morocco to Asia in great detail. One of the earliest writers in Europe was Petrarch, who wrote about his ascent of Mount Ventoux in 1336, describing his travelling companions who stayed at the bottom as *frigida incuriositas*, meaning they had a 'cold lack of curiosity'.

You may have read quite a lot of travel writing, but now you are moving on to a higher level in your English studies you need to start to think more deeply about *how and why* a text is written, and how specific words are selected to affect the reader.

Summit of Mount Ventoux, France

Carry out the following activities.

1. Read this account of a visit to Venezuela printed in a daily newspaper. Make notes on what it tells you about:

   a the writer

   b how the writer has informed and entertained her readers

   c how readers may have reacted to information in the article.

2. Carry out some online or library research into Christopher Columbus or Walter Raleigh, and make a list of **people**, **places** and **things** they discovered on their explorations.

Children of the Stars

1   Los Roques is a coral archipelago 150 km off the coast of Venezuela consisting of 42 small islands surrounding a huge lagoon. Here, in this paradisiacal playground, hurricanes hardly happen. The days are hot and the nights are cool. Venezuelans
5   visit at weekends to snorkel, scuba dive and watch the sunset, returning to Gran Roque, the only inhabited island, for dinner and a comfortable night in one of the many delightful *posadas*.

Following in the wake of Christopher Columbus and Walter Raleigh, we took a boat up the Orinoco River. Our guides
10 encouraged us to take a dip in the river at sunset. It looked inviting – the wide dark waters tinged with pink, parrots winging their way home above a wall of green jungle. A young Belgian couple took the plunge. But are there crocodiles? And piranha fish? Yes! But there are also electric-blue morph

15 butterflies with wings as large as your hand, noisy families of red howler monkeys and the part-reptile guacharaca bird, a hang-over from pre-historic times.

There was also plenty of wildlife activity at the jungle camp. A magnificent puma, brought in as baby by the Indians, paced
20 the length of its enclosure. In the rafters of the dining room an **ocelot** and a racoon played together while a family of otters honked noisily for scraps at our table. A huge tarantula sitting on an adjacent banana plant caused a stir. The young Belgian took it on the back of his hand but his mosquito repellent irritated
25 the spider which slowly 'hunched up', a sign that it was ready to deliver its poison, our guide gently coaxed it back to its leaf – no harm done!

The Orinoco delta is home to the Warao Indians. The river is their highway and the canoe their only mode of transport. (...)
30 The Warao believe they came from the stars and their god brought them to the Orinoco Delta, to paradise, where the Mareche, the 'tree of life', grow in abundance. The Mareche produces an orange fruit which, when softened for several days, makes a **palatable** juice (...). The young tree yields a string from
35 which hammocks and baskets are made. When the tree rots it is home to a large, yellow grub, an excellent source of protein – eaten live. I was offered a chance to try this wriggling delicacy – I just wasn't hungry!

From *Children of the Stars* by Angela Clarence,
The *Observer* (5 November 2000)

Word cloud

ocelot
palatable
posadas

Pathways – going places

✎ Choosing a holiday destination

Advertisements are written to inform and persuade. Read these two advertisements for very different cities and do the directed writing activity that follows.

Historic Venice

1   Mists and masked balls in palace and piazza, romance, pageant and splendour. Take a step out of reality and enjoy five unforgettable days in romantic, historic Venice.

Perhaps you think you know it already. You've seen the Bond
5   movies, the ads featuring gondoliers steering enraptured tourists along the Grand Canal. But Venice is far more than picturesque bridges. Come and discover its hidden corners. Take a turn through historic streets, see its architecture and experience its other-worldly atmosphere. Wander the City of Water with a loved
10 one or join a group walk with an experienced guide, who'll tell you about Canaletto and the peccadilloes of the wicked Lord Byron.

Stop to listen to a string quartet, drink the best espresso as you wait for your vaporetto, take a trip to Murano or wander through colourful street markets. And then, when you've found
15 the real Venice, see the Bridge of Sighs, the Doge's Palace, the Piazza San Marco and the Rialto Bridge. And make sure to visit an original Venetian glass factory to choose a keepsake forever – for this is a holiday to remember – for ever.

Once a powerful state, home to bankers and speculators, Venice
20 was an influential player in world politics. It is now a UNESCO World Heritage Site and the most delightful car-free zone in Europe. But Venice is under threat from rising water levels. Be sure to see this enchanting City of Light, before it's too late!

NEW YORK, NEW YORK!

1   New York City is a heady blend of iconic images, eclectic neighbourhoods and community spirit and no other place in the world will give you such a strong feeling of déjà vu.

Yellow cabs, steaming vents and towering buildings provide
5   a continuous reminder of where you are and the unique personality of a typical New Yorker has got to be experienced first-hand.

No matter whether you're taking a stroll through Central Park, marvelling at the money monuments on Wall Street or simply enjoying a lazy brunch at one of the easy-going diners, New York City really does have something for everyone.

The layout of the city makes navigation straight forward and all the major suburbs can be visited via bus, cab or on foot. From Manhattan to China Town; Little Italy to Brooklyn, New York is one destination that you'll want to visit time and time again.

Eats and drinks

There are thousands of restaurants in this city representing every type of cooking possible. 21 Club is a New York institute, as is Diner, a converted dining car with a loyal clientele. Chat 'n' Chew, just off Union Square, is a heartland eatery where people chat as they wait to chew on gooey, piping hot macaroni cheese or a mountainous burger!

From a sales advertisement,
Virgin Holidays Ltd.

Writing to persuade

You are planning your summer vacation. Your friend has suggested the locations in the advertisements on these two pages.

Write an email to your friend telling him or her which city you prefer, Venice or New York.

Persuade them your choice is the better option. Use information from the advertisements to support your answer.

Write about 250–300 words. Include the following:

- what makes the location special
- why the other location is less appealing
- sample itinerary, day trips and local attractions
- why the location is a good choice for students of your age.

Pathways – going places

💬 Creating a holiday advertisement

You work for an advertising agency and you have been asked to create a newspaper and television advertisement for an amazing new holiday location.

Your team at the agency are all on holiday at the moment, leaving you with the following roles to perform – and a deadline to meet – all on your own!

- Art director (responsible for illustrations and images)
- Copy editor (responsible for checking text is accurate in the final versions of the advertisements)
- Copy writer (who creates original written material)
- Video director
- Voice actor(s)
- Other roles you think necessary
- Legal expert to check copyright and photograph permissions.

Complete the following activities.

1. Decide on your 'amazing holiday location' and create the following:
   a A full colour advertisement for newspapers and magazines (Hint: you can use the advertisements on these pages and the previous pages to help you).
   b The script for the television advertisement (maximum 2 minutes).

2. Collaborate with your classmates to make a video of the advertisement for television, or to be performed in front of the rest of the class.

3. Consider the ideas that your classmates came up with.
   a Can you identify any common themes?
   b Which advertising technique did you find most effective, and why?

Antarctica Expedition

1 The adventure of an Antarctic expedition is the ultimate holiday experience. The 7th continent, Antarctica, is for many the ultimate wilderness destination – a pristine area navigable only by small specially ice-strengthened vessels.

Until recently, Antarctica was accessible only to the men and women of meticulously planned pioneering expeditions. However, following strict environmental guidelines, small groups on expedition vessels can now follow in the footsteps of those explorers and navigate through sea-sculpted bergs and groaning, crumbling glaciers to discover sights rarely seen by humanity.

During the short summer months the vast pack ice opens and this often harsh and inhospitable environment plays host to one of the greatest wildlife spectacles on earth. Millions of penguins, petrels and albatrosses breed here, seals laze languidly on ice floes, and whales indulge Zodiacs benignly under virtual 24-hour daylight.

Some choose the Peninsula, others further afield to the Circle and those with more time may visit the wildlife strongholds of the Falklands and especially South Georgia. Whatever the decision, this wilderness, seen from a small expedition vessel, not a monstrous cruise ship, will attract and enchant like no other.

From a sales advertisement,
Exodus Travels Ltd

Spice Island Adventure: INDONESIA

Cloves and nutmeg, rainforests and ruins, volcanoes and golden sand

Experience Java's enigmatic ruins and visit the World Heritage site of Borobudur. Discover tiny islands crammed with sweet-smelling spices, see orang-utans in their primal jungles; chill out on verandas under volcanoes; take boat trips to visit cultures unknown, and eat exquisite rice dishes. Stretch out on paradisiacal beaches in Bali and gaze at the glorious sunset. Each of Indonesia's islands has something different and special. Spice Island Adventures offers a ten day trip that will take you through jungle wilderness and past fascinating sites of human civilisation. You'll see biodiversity in action, golden beaches and places where magic and mystery are at the heart of daily life.

Sample itinerary: Start Jakarta.

Day 2: Drive to Yogyakarta and visit Borobudur Heritage site.

Day 3: Bali – a day on the beach and a night of luxury.

Day 4: Set sail on the Banda Sea.

Days 5–8: Visit unmapped islands and see the magic of Indonesia...

Haoyou is a 12-year-old boy whose story is set in China in the 13th century. Hayou's father, a sailor, has been killed in an accident when he was forced to fly as a human kite 'testing the wind' for a sailing ship. Haoyou must now provide an income for his mother and baby sister. His older cousin Mipeng helps him to overcome his fears.

The Kite-maker

So Haoyou became a kite-maker. Haoyou the artisan. Haoyou the breadwinner. Great-Uncle Bo (…), grudgingly gave money enough to buy some lengths of reject silk, some soiled paper, sewing thread, size, and a craft knife. Haoyou went out himself to cut bamboo, which he split into spills. He made red kites and blue ones, white kites and yellow.

'Where shall I put them?' he asked his mother, holding up the first, moving his hand back and forth so that the size-wet silk breathed like a diaphragm.

'In your father's bedroom,' said Qing'an. 'I'll sleep by the hearth.' Haoyou was shocked that his model-making should oust his mother from her bed, but obedience forbade him to argue. Besides, his heart thrilled at the thought his kites were adjudged so important. Up until now, they had simply been a hobby. Now they were his profession, and his mother walked among them as through a zoo of weird and wonderful animals.

As indeed, they were.

Haoyou made triangular kites and square ones, oblongs and pennons with swallow tails. He made box kites and tubular kites, and with every one, he mastered some new deftness, learned some secret trick of quickness, and how to keep waste to the minimum.

His friends said, 'Let's see what you made, Haoyou! Let's see.' But Haoyou only smiled that polite, businessman's smile which he had seen Great-Uncle Bo use: the yes which meant no. 'When I have enough,' he told them.

His mother—quiet-spoken at the best of times—trod the house as hesitantly as a crane, and said nothing. But he heard her murmur to the family shrine, where Pei's rice bowl stood, 'Do you see, Pei? Do you see how hard our boy is working?' And then the pride and honour pricked behind

Haoyou's eyes and he vowed to make the most beautiful kites Dagu had ever seen.

He made kites in the shape of fish and kites in the shape of dragons: (...) big rats with long tails of string. He painted them with lucky words and propitious numbers copied from over rich men's doors. He could not read himself, but he knew the importance of good luck symbols. Then, as each was finished, he carried it through to the bedroom and found a place for it among the rest. He kept the door-hanging drawn at all times, so that no one should see his stock before he was ready to show it.

'When will you start to sell them?' asked his mother, though for two months she had held her tongue.

'When I have enough,' said Haoyou, hoping to sound like his father, incontrovertible. His mother's eyes sank to the floor, but not in trusting submission, only sadness. All of Great-Uncle Bo's money had gone, and there was none left to buy rice. All the chickens had gone out of the coop. There was nothing left. (...)

Then, who should call at the house but Mipeng. It seemed that mere chance had brought her; Haoyou did not hear his mother whisper, as she embraced the visitor, 'Thank you for coming; I didn't know who else to ask.'

Tea was fetched—the last dusty scrapings from the bottom of the caddy. Qing'an blushed with shame at the lack of rice cakes. But Mipeng did not seem even to notice. Qing'an praised her son's handiwork, and Mipeng naturally asked to see the finished kites.

Since the curtain still lay torn from its hangings, there was nothing Haoyou could do to stop her pattering demurely into his private preserve. He groaned inwardly. Now she would marvel at his cleverness and craftsmanship. Haoyou squirmed. He never knew how to answer compliments.

But all Mipeng said was, 'Do they fly?'

'Well, yes. Of course. I suppose,' said Haoyou, rather taken aback.

'You can't sell them unless they fly.'

Haoyou had been making kites ever since he was old enough to tell a bowl of glue apart from his breakfast. He was rather offended. 'If they don't fly, people can bring them back. I'll give them their money back,' he said.

Modern Banyao kite making in Nantong, China

Mipeng picked up a great dragony box kite with a trailing tail. 'Wouldn't it be better to test them yourself?'

'No!' He took the kite out of her hands. 'If they crashed, I'd have nothing to sell.'

'If they crash you will have no customers after the first week.' And she took the kite back out of his hand, posting it through the narrow doorway and out into the living room. 'Let's go and test this one.'

'I suppose you are waiting for the Boys' Festival,' Mipeng called over her shoulder, moving with remarkable speed, given the steepness of the hill and the unsuitability of her clothes. The hill was busy with children bundled up in six layers of tattered clothing and sent by their mothers to breathe in the wholesome air. (In point of fact, the air carried oily reminders of the fish-gutting tables on the waterfront, and the wind was bitter.)

The Boys' Festival was an annual outing taken by families with thriving sons, to celebrate their good fortune and bring the boys good health and good luck. A boy with his face turned up to the sky looses all the stale vapours from his body.

He enjoys himself, too.

Haoyou had never given the Boys' Festival a thought, but he said, 'Yes, yes. That's what I thought. The Boys' Festival... when is it?'

Mipeng looked sidelong at him again out of those astonishing coal-black eyes. 'Next month. In the meantime, if you and your mother and sister can learn to eat air, like the dragons, all will be well.'

Above them, on the skyline, a sprinkling of kites hung in the sky like lazy hawks. The higher Haoyou climbed, the stronger the wind blew. The kite, which they were carrying between them, began to wriggle and buck, as if eager to be chasing the other, puny kites across the sky.

'Oh dear,' said Haoyou. 'I forgot the string.'

'I didn't,' said Mipeng and drew out a bobbin of cord and attached it to the dragon.

But Haoyou's legs would not take him any further. His knees were shaking. His palms were wet. 'I can't,' he said. 'Don't make me. Please.'

If he pitched his kite into the wind, he would have to watch it all over again—that hatch-cover lifting into the air, his father's hair spread out against the woven rushes, that mouth shouting out his name, the spittle like silver between taut lips, those hands and feet rigid as bird talons. 'I can't,' he said. 'Honoured father's up there.'

'So?'

Even through his fright, Haoyou was startled by this odd young woman.

'Why did you have to say I'd make kites?' he roared, bursting into tears. 'Why kites of all things? Father wouldn't want me to make kites! Not kites of all things!'

The louder he shouted, the softer Mipeng spoke. 'What else can a boy with clever hands make from cheap materials? Great-Uncle Bo is not a generous man. Would you prefer I'd said your mother ought to marry the tattooed sailor?' She lifted the dragon's boxy head and appeared to be about to hurl it at him. Haoyou ducked. With a noise like a string of paper lanterns in a hurricane, the dragon swallowed the wind, reared up and thrashed into the air. The other children on the hill gave a single cry of admiration and dropped their fists, so that their kites staggered in the sky. Up went the dragon, bucking and undulating, shedding a paper scale or two from its long, fragile body. The string reeled off its bobbin with a poppety-poppety-popping. Both their heads went back: the wind was cold in Haoyou's throat. Lunging through a great figure of eight, the dragon-kite gulped in the wind and struggled skywards. One of the bamboo joints came unglued; next time Haoyou would have to use more thread to reinforce it. The tail swished. The other children on the hill gave a groan of longing. To own such a kite!

Mipeng tried to pass Haoyou the bobbin, but he snatched his hands away.

'Why? What are you afraid of?'

'Of him!' hissed Haoyou, pointing at the sky. A hilltop was no place to whisper and he had to say it again. *'Of him! He's up there!'*

'Your father?' she shouted it into the teeth of the wind. 'Well? He loved you when he was alive, didn't he? Why shouldn't he love you now?'

Haoyou's hands turned into two little fists. *'Because I let them do that to him! Because I didn't stop them! Because I didn't help him! I didn't stop them!'*

Slowly, gradually, Mipeng moved round behind him, looping her arms over his head so that the bobbin was in front of him. The circle of her arms gripped his shoulders. 'Listen. There's nothing you could have done, Haoyou. Nothing. Nothing. Di Chou wanted your father dead, because he wants your mother for himself. Nothing you could have done would have stopped him killing Pei.'

Haoyou's heart lurched into his mouth. 'How do you . . . ?'

'We've met, Di Chou and I.'

The sky spun round. Haoyou took hold of the bobbin just to keep himself from falling. He knew instantly that every word was true. (...)

'Didn't I tell you the man was dangerous?' she said. 'He's set his heart on having Qing'an. He told me what to predict at the seance. A marriage for her. A new father for you. He didn't take it kindly when I said something different.'

Then Haoyou forgot all about the dragon tugging on his arms. A wave of hatred went through him too big for his chest to hold. He saw it as clearly as if he, and not Mipeng, was the clairvoyant. He saw that great ox of a man lurking in the alleyway, waiting his chance, stepping out of the shadows as Mipeng made her way home one night (...)

'And he hasn't given up, you know,' said Mipeng. 'He's only waiting for you to fail. You must be very careful of that one.'

The dragon-kite bounded about the sky, roaring its hatred of First Mate Di Chou, pawing the air. The other children on the hill were yelling at Haoyou now: *'Where did you get it?'*

'Did you make it?'

'How much did it cost?'

'I'm going to ask my brother to buy me one!'

'I won't fail,' he said between gritted teeth. 'I'll be the greatest kite-maker in all Dagu. In all Cathay!' He turned his face upwards towards the sky, opening his mouth wide to catch the air, just as the dragon kite was doing.

'Where did you get it?'

'How much? How much?'

'I'm going to ask my uncle to buy . . .'

'Where can we buy . . . ?'

'At my house,' Haoyou yelled back above the noise of the blustery wind. 'Plenty more like this one. Very good prices. You want to buy this one? It's for sale.'

The little boys reeled in their kites and ran home to ask their parents for money to buy a kite like the one they had seen on the hill. The dragon took longer to fetch down—it had climbed so high and resisted capture now that it had tasted freedom.

From *The Kite Rider* by Geraldine McCaughrean

Understanding

1. Why is Haoyou scared of flying his kite?
2. Who is Di Chou, and why does Mipeng think that he is dangerous?
3. From this text, what can you tell about the following people's character? Use examples to support your answer.
   a Haoyou
   b His mother, Qing'an
   c His cousin, Mipeng
   d His Great-Uncle Bo

Extension

1. How does the writer build up your knowledge of the characters? Use examples to support your answer.
2. Chinese customs and beliefs from the 13th century are referred to in this extract, some of which exist to this day.
   a What are these beliefs and customs? How are they presented?
   b How do the beliefs and customs in this story compare to those of your own country?
3. You are a time-traveller who has gone to visit Haoyou in 13th century China. Write a diary entry or a travel blog about your adventure. Use the text extracts in Unit 10 to help you.

Language and literacy reference

Active voice versus passive voice – Verbs are active when the subject of the sentence (the agent) does the action. Example: The shark swallowed the fish. Active verbs are used more in informal speech or writing.

Verbs are passive when the subject of the sentence has the action done to it. Example: The fish was swallowed by the shark. Passive verbs are used in more formal writing such as reports. Examples: An eye-witness was interviewed by the police. Results have been analysed by the sales team.

Sometimes turning an active sentence to passive, or vice versa, simply means moving the agent:

- The shark (agent and subject) + verb = active
- The fish (object) + verb = passive

Adjective – An adjective describes a noun or adds to its meaning. They are usually found in front of a noun. Example: Green emeralds and glittering diamonds. Adjectives can also come after a verb. Examples: It was big. They looked hungry. Sometimes you can use two adjectives together. Example: tall and handsome. This is called an adjectival phrase.

Adjectives can be used to describe degrees of intensity. To make a comparative adjective you usually add –er (or use more). Examples: quicker; more beautiful. To make a superlative you add –est (or use most). Examples: quickest; most beautiful.

Adverb – An adverb adds further meaning to a verb. Many are formed by adding -ly to an adjective. Example: slow/slowly. They often come next to the verb in a sentence. Adverbs can tell the reader: how – quickly, stupidly, amazingly; where – there, here, everywhere; when – yesterday, today, now; how often – occasionally, often.

Adverbial phrase – The part of a sentence that tells the reader when, where or how something happens is called an adverbial phrase. It is a group of words that functions as an adverb. Example: I'm going to the dentist **tomorrow morning** (when); The teacher spoke to us **as if he was in a bad mood** (how); Sam ran **all the way home** (where). These adverbials are called adverbials of time, manner and place.

Alliteration – Alliteration occurs when two or more nearby words start with the same sound. Example: A slow, sad, sorrowful song.

Antecedent – An antecedent is the person or thing to which the pronoun refers back. Example: President Alkira realised that his life was in danger. 'President Alkira' is the antecedent here.

Antonym – An antonym is a word or phrase that means the opposite of another word or phrase in the same language. Example: shut is an antonym of open. Synonyms and antonyms can be used to add variation and depth to your writing.

Audience – The readers of a text and/or the people for whom the author is writing; the term can also apply to those who watch a film or to television viewers.

Clause – A clause is a group of words that contains a subject and a verb. Example: I ran. In this clause, I is the subject and ran is the verb.

Cliché – An expression, idiom or phrase that has been repeated so often it has lost its significance.

Colloquial language – Informal, everyday speech as used in conversation; it may include slang expressions. Not appropriate in written reports, essays or exams.

Colon – A colon is a punctuation mark (:) used to indicate an example, explanation or list is being used by the writer within the sentence. Examples: You will need: a notebook, a pencil, a notepad and a ruler. I am quick at running: as fast as a cheetah.

Conjugate – To change the tense or subject of a verb.

Conditional tense – This tense is used to talk about something that might happen. Conditionals are sometimes called 'if' clauses. They can be used to talk imaginary situations or possible real-life scenarios. Examples: If it gets any colder the river will freeze. If I had a million pounds I would buy a zoo.

Conjunction – A conjunction is a word used to link clauses within a sentence such as: and, but, so, until, when, as. Example: He had a book in his hand when he stood up.

Connectives – A connective is a word or a phrase that links clauses or sentences. Connectives can be conjunctions. Example: but, when, because. Connectives can also be connecting adverbs. Example: then, therefore, finally.

Continuous tense – This tense is used to tell you that something is continuing to happen. Example: I am watching football.

Discourse markers – Words and phrases such as on the other hand, to sum up, however, and therefore are called discourse markers because they mark stages along an argument. Using them will make your paragraphs clearer and more orderly.

Exclamation – An exclamation shows someone's feelings about something. Example: What a pity!

Exclamation mark – An exclamation mark makes a phrase or a short sentence stand out. You usually use it in phrases like 'How silly I am!' and more freely in dialogue when people are speaking. Don't use it at the end of a long, factual sentence, and don't use it too often.

Idiom – An idiom is a colourful expression which has become fixed in the language. It is a phrase which has a meaning that cannot be worked out from the meanings of the words in it. Examples: 'in hot water' means 'in trouble'; It's raining cats and dogs.

Imagery – A picture in words, often using a metaphor or simile (figurative language) which describes something in detail: writers use visual, aural (auditory) or tactile imagery to convey how something looks, sounds or feels in all forms of writing, not just fiction or poetry. Imagery helps the reader to feel like they are actually there.

Irregular verb – An irregular verb does not follow the standard grammatical rules. Each has to be learned as it does not follow any pattern. For example, catch becomes caught in the past tense, not catched.

Metaphor – A metaphor is a figure of speech in which one thing is actually said to be the other. Example: This man is a lion in battle.

Non-restrictive clause – A non-restrictive clause provides additional information about a noun. They can be taken away from the sentence and it will still make sense. They are separated from the rest of the sentence by commas (or brackets). Example: The principal, who liked order, was shocked and angry.

Onomatopoeia – Words that imitate sounds, sensations or textures. Example: bang, crash, prickly, squishy.

Paragraph – A group of sentences (minimum of two, except in modern fiction) linked by a single idea or subject. Each paragraph should contain a topic sentence. Paragraphs should be planned, linked and organised to lead up to a conclusion in most forms of writing.

Parenthetical phrase – A parenthetical phrase is a phrase that has been added into a sentence which is already complete, to provide additional information. It is usually separated from other clauses using a pair of commas or a pair of brackets (parentheses). Examples: The leading goal scorer at the 2014 World Cup – James Rodriguez, playing for Columbia – scored five goals. The leading actor in the film, Hollywood great Gene Kelly, is captivating.

Passive voice – See active voice.

Person (first, second or third) – The first person is used to talk about oneself – I/we. The second person is used to address the person who is listening or reading – you. The third person is used to refer to someone else – he, she, it, they.

- I feel like I've been here for days. (first person)
- Look what you get, when you join the club. (second person)
- He says it takes real courage. (third person)

Personification – Personification can work at two levels: it can give an animal the characteristics of a human, and it can give an abstract thing the characteristics of a human or an animal. Example: I was looking Death in the face.

Prefix – A prefix is an element placed at the beginning of a word to modify its meaning. Prefixes include: dis-, un-, im-, in-, il-, ir-.
Examples: impossible, inconvenient, irresponsible.

Preposition – A preposition is a word that indicates place (on, in), direction (over, beyond) or time (during, on) among others.

Pronoun – A pronoun is a word that can replace a noun, often to avoid repetition. Example: I put the book on the table. It was next to the plant. 'It' refers back to the book in first sentence.

- Subject pronouns act as the subject of the sentence: I, you, he, she, it.
- Object pronouns act as the object of the sentence: me, you, him, her, it, us, you, them.
- Possessive pronouns how that something belongs to someone: mine, yours, his, hers, its, ours, yours, theirs.
- Demonstrative pronouns refer to things: this, that, those, these.

Questions – There are different types of questions.

- Closed questions – This type of question can be answered with a single-word response, can be answered with 'yes' or 'no', can be answered by choosing from a list of possible answers and identifies a piece of specific information.
- Open questions – This type of question cannot be answered with a single-word response, it requires a more thoughtful answer than just 'yes' or 'no'.
- Leading questions – This type of question suggests what answer should be given. Example: Why are robot servants bad for humans? This suggests to the responder that robots are bad as the question is "why are they bad?" rather than "do you think they are bad?" Also called loaded questions.
- Rhetorical question – Rhetorical questions are questions that do not require an answer but serve to give the speaker an excuse to explain his/her views. Rhetorical questions should be avoided in formal writing and essays. Example: Who wouldn't want to go on holiday?

Register – The appropriate style and tone of language chosen for a specific purpose and/or audience. When speaking to your friends and family you use an informal register whereas you use a more formal tone if talking to someone older, in a position of authority or who you do not know very well. Example: I'm going to do up the new place.

(informal) I am planning to decorate my new flat. (more formal)

Regular verb – A regular verb follows the rules when conjugated (e.g. by adding –ed in the past tense, such as walk which becomes walked).

Relative clause – Relative clauses are a type of subordinate clause. They describe or explain something that has just been mentioned using who, whose, which, where, whom, that, or when. Example: The girl who was standing next to the counter was carrying a small dog.

Relative pronoun – A relative pronoun does what it says – it takes an idea and relates it to a person or a thing. Be careful to use 'who' for people and 'which' for things. Example: I talked to your teacher, who told me about your unfinished homework. This is my favourite photo, which shows you the beach and the palm trees.

Restrictive clause – Restrictive clauses identify the person or thing that is being referred to and are vital to the meaning of the sentence. They are not separated from the rest of the sentence by a comma. With restrictive clauses, you can often drop the relative pronoun. Example: The letter [that] I wrote yesterday was lost.

Semi-colon – A semi-colon is a punctuation mark (;) that separates two main clauses. It is stronger than a comma but not as strong as a full stop. Each clause could form a sentence by itself. Example: I like cheese; it is delicious.

Sentence – A sentence is a group of words that expresses a complete thought. All sentences begin with a capital letter and end with a full stop, question mark or exclamation mark.

- Simple sentences are made up of one clause. Example: I am hungry.
- Complex sentence – Complex sentences are made up of one main clause and one, or more, subordinate clauses. A subordinate clause cannot stand on its own and relies on the main clause. Example: When I joined the drama club, I did not know that it was going to be so much fun.
- Compound sentence – Compound sentences are made up of two or more main clauses, usually joined by a conjunction. Example: I am hungry and I am thirsty.

Good writers use sentences of different lengths to vary the pace of their writing. Short sentences can make a strong impact while longer sentences can make text flow.

Simile – A simile is a figure of speech in which two things are compared using the linking words 'like' or 'as'. Example: In battle, he was as brave as a lion.

Simple past tense – This tense us used to tell you that something happened in the past. Only one verb is required. Example: I wore.

Simple present tense – This tense is used to tell you that something is happening now. Only one verb is required. Example: I wear.

Standard English – Standard English is the form of English used in most writing and by educated speakers. It can be spoken with any accent. There are many slight differences between Standard English and local ways of speaking. Example: 'We were robbed' is Standard English but in speech some people say, 'We was robbed.'

Suffix – A suffix is an element placed at the end of a word to modify its meaning. Suffixes include: -ible, -able, -ful, -less. Example: useful, useless, meaningful, meaningless.

Summary – A summary is a record of the main points of something you have read, seen or heard. Keep to the point and keep it short. Use your own words to make everything clear.

Synonym – A synonym is a word or phrase that means nearly the same as another word or phrase in the same language. Example: shut is a synonym of close. Synonyms and antonyms can be used to add variation and depth to your writing.

Syntax – The study of how words are organised in a sentence.

Tense – A tense is a verb form that shows whether events happen in the past, present or the future.

- The Pyramids are on the west bank of the River Nile. (present tense)
- They were built as enormous tombs. (past tense)
- They will stand for centuries to come. (future tense)

Most verbs change their spelling by adding –ed to form the past tense. Example: walk/walked. Some have irregular spellings. Example: catch/caught.

Topic sentence – The key sentence of a paragraph that contains the principal idea or subject being discussed.